ROBOTNIK

A SHORT HISTORY OF THE STRUGGLE FOR WORKER SELF-MANAGEMENT AND FREE TRADE UNIONS IN POLAND, 1944–1981

DAVID R. STEFANCIC

EAST EUROPEAN MONOGRAPHS, BOULDER
DISTRIBUTED BY COLUMBIA UNIVERSITY PRESS, NEW YORK

1992

EAST EUROPEAN MONOGRAPHS, NO. CCCXXXVIII

Copyright 1992 by David R. Stefancic
ISBN 0-88033-235-2
Library of Congress Catalog Card Number 91-78353

Printed in the United States of America

Contents

Foreword   v

Introduction   v

Chapter One   We Need More Discipline   1

Chapter Two   We Are Workers Not Hooligans . . .   21

Chapter Three   Three Together Make Revolution . .   38

Chapter Four   We Are Not Comrades, We Are Citizens!   56

Chapter Five   To Mix Fire and Water   74

Chapter Six   Saddling the Cow   90

Epilogue   97

Notes   99

Bibliography   107

Introduction

In the summer of 1980 the world was stunned by the creation of an entity that to this point in history was unheard and unthought of. The existence of an independent trade union in a Marxist-Leninist state attracted the curiosity of many. The trade union, Solidarity, had been looked at from many viewpoints. It has been viewed from the stand of the Party, the intelligentsia, and the Catholic Church, but little has been done to look at this phenomena from the level of the workers. This was a workers' trade union founded by workers, organized by workers, and run by workers. They were and are searching for democracy in a worker's state.

The objective of this study is to place Solidarity into a historical context by looking at the development of the Polish working class since the end of World War II. To be more specific, I will trace two trends that are evident in the Polish labor movement; one towards autonomous trade unionism and the other centered around the concept of worker self-management. They both have been evident in the workers' movement since 1944 and eventually surfaced to their greatest extent with the creation of Solidarity in 1980 and the Network (Siec) of Solidarity Organizations in Leading Factories. Both trends have survived martial law and exist in Poland today.

Another aspect of this study is to look at the continuity of the workers' movement over the past four decades. Writers have tended to look at the 1970s as the source of the workers' protest, but this is a very limited view and fails to take into account the continuity within the movement from 1944 and earlier to the present Solidarity organization.

This is a history of the Polish working class from 1944 to 1981. To make this history complete, it would take many years and many volumes. To make this topic more manageable, several limiting factors had to be introduced to the study. To emphasize the worker aspect of this history, I have tended to deemphasize certain periods of Polish political and religious history that would be important in a larger study but are not necessary for a study of such limited scope. When I use the term worker I mean the urban blue collar variety and have left white collar and rural labor for future research.

This study is divided into six chapters and is meant to show continuity rather than episodes in history. It is also meant to show how the present is nothing more than a progression of the past.

Acknowledgements

This work is dedicated to a variety of people who have influenced its final outcome. I want to thank Dr. Waclaw Soroka, Dr. M.K. Dziewanowski, Dr. Fred Kremple, Dr. Roland Stromberg, Dr. Vatro Murvar, Dr. Neal Pease, and Dr. Jack McGovern for their suggestions and support in the undertaking of this project. They have instilled in me a love of history, made me a better researcher, and most importantly, have provided me with prime examples of how to be a good teacher. I want to thank my family and friends for their support and encouragement. I most of all want to thank my wife, Pam, who has been the most important source of support in my life for the last fifteen years.

Chapter One

We Need More Discipline

The year 1944 was a period of dramatic changes for Poland. The Polish people were throwing off almost five years of a brutal Nazi occupation only to have it replaced with a new occupier from the East. These new Soviet "liberators" were not only freeing Poland from their Nazi captor but were also bringing with them a new political, economic, and social system. This new world was to be presented to the Poles not at their request but at the insistence of their new "friends." At no time was this imposition of a new system more evident than during the Warsaw Uprising of 1944. The Soviet response to the battle of Warsaw was to show that they were not interested in restoring an independent Poland but creating a satellite state.

In the summer of 1944, the German army was in retreat on the Eastern front. The Red Army was in full pursuit and pushing the beleaguered Germans toward the Polish capitol of Warsaw. The Polish underground army prepared to aid the Russian army by starting an armed uprising within Warsaw. The objectives of the uprising were to save the city from total destruction and to free the city before the Russians arrived. The underground wanted to achieve a moral victory by regaining their own capitol and give the appearance of being masters in their own house. The Polish underground army or Home Army was allied to the government in exile in London which was opposed to many of the changes that the Soviets had in mind for the new Poland. The Red Army had little intention of aiding a group of armed insurgents that would be opposed to them later.

On August 1, the city of Warsaw struck out at a surprised German army. Despite early successes, the Home Army needed the assistance of the Soviet army if victory was to occur. The Red Army refused to aid the insurgents and prevented the Americans and the

British from aiding them. The fighting lasted for two months before the Poles surrendered with their city destroyed and over 200,000 casualties. The last bastion of the prewar government had been neutralized and the way had been cleared for a new government; the Soviet-sponsored Committee of Polish Patriots.

Despite the shift of governments, the Poles, in 1944 and 1945, were mostly concerned with rebuilding their war-ravaged land and getting on with their lives. They would resist the new order, if possible, but the key objective was to get the Polish nation on a sound footing again. Each social group took upon itself to do what it could to rebuild a new Poland from what was left after the German occupation. The Workers were to take a leading role in this rebuilding process.

As the German army pulled out of Poland and the Red Army moved in, the Polish people were faced with a very difficult task ahead of them. They had to rebuild a country in which almost every city was devastated, a fourth of the prewar population was missing, and 60 percent of all industry was destroyed. The people responded to these problems by attacking those most closely related to them; keeping the remaining industry going or restarting production where possible. The new Provisional Government (the Committee of Polish Patriots) was incapable of doing this on its own since it was still fighting the Germans.

Workers' committees began to form in the newly liberated territories as soon as the German army left. No one was left to run the factories since the prewar owners were either dead or in exile and the most recent owners were fleeing back to the Fatherland. The Provisional Government was more than willing to hand over control of the factories to the workers but only for a short while. Many of the workers' committees had operated since 1939 in the underground and began to operate in the open when it was safe to do so. The committees' first objective was to elect leaders who were to take the place of factory management.

The workers took it upon themselves to rebuild their enterprises and track down the necessary raw materials to keep the factories functioning. Machinery was repaired or salvaged from destroyed factories. People were recruited to work and production goals were set. For protection of the factories, a workers' militia was formed. The activities that the workers engaged in were not unusual or unfamiliar to them. They had watched these actions go on around them and had even participated in some of them prior to this point in time. The unusual step taken by the workers was that now they were in charge of directing these tasks in addition to just carrying them out. They now had the dual function of being the director and worker in an enterprise. This arrangement worked relatively smoothly until the new government began to take charge of the situation.[1]

The workers' committees took it upon themselves to inform the new authorities of their activities when the time was appropriate. The Provisional Government was pleased to see the initiative of the workers in regard to the take over and the operation of the remaining factories. The workers' actions fit in quite well with the ideological outlook of the new rulers of Poland. The new government was more than happy to transfer some of their responsibilities for the economy to other groups until they could secure their own position. In fact, the activity of the workers had caught them by surprise. The Manifesto of the Provisional Government, issued on July 22, 1944, made no mention of workers' control of enterprises or factory committees. Worker management had been a major plank in the program of the Polish Workers Party (communist) until it came to power. The authorities had hoped to work out some arrangement after the war by which some private business would be allowed to reopen under the prewar owners. This idea was abandoned in the light of the worker's actions. The July Manifesto stated that the local authorities and the worker's committee would secure deserted factories. They made no mention of the workers taking over and running an abandoned enterprise. The Provisional Government was not happy with some of the autonomy; these were quickly dissolved. It was not until October of 1944 that the government issued a decree on the worker's committees. The authorities decided to recognize some of the committees and give them a limited role in the new system. The workers were to share the management duties of an enterprise with the director and the local authorities. The decree provided no clear cut lines of power, creating constant confusion over who was in charge. The workers had different objectives than those of the directors or government representatives. The workers tended to stress short range goals for production and an egalitarian approach toward wages. The authorities had grandiose schemes of making Poland a viable part of the new socialist system as soon as possible and the workers' living conditions were not top priority. The first major experiment in workers' councils in Poland was to be over by the spring of 1945.[2]

In February of 1945, the powers of the workers' councils were delineated. The government decided that a workers' representative was to have a permanent seat on the managerial board of industrial enterprises. This representative was to be drawn from the worker's councils. The councils also were to be active in the selection of new management, the setting of production goals and pay scales. These powers were defended by Hilary Minc, minister of industry, as a way of increasing the productivity of Polish workers. The councils were to make the workers feel as if they really were an active part of the new social order. This temporary expansion of the workers' councils' powers led to the further frustration of the newly appointed industrial managers. No one knew who precisely was in charge; the councils or the managers. There was continual friction over incentives and bonuses between the councils and management. Management wanted to link incentives and bonuses to productivity and skills while the councils demanded an equal cut for all. Some councils went so far as to suggest the elimination of bonuses for non-manual personnel (management). This suggestion went too far. Directors began to level formal complaints against the councils as roadblocks to efficiency. The government quietly began to rescind many of the powers that they had just given to the councils. The workers were starting to show signs of syndicalism and this did not fit into the plans for centralization that the Party was preparing for the economy. The Party began to see in the workers' councils a potential rival power base. The time had come to deal with this possible threat before it got out of hand.[3]

By May of 1945, the Central Committee of the Polish Workers Party decided to take further steps to increase productivity and end the anarchistic trends in the workers' councils. A conflict between the councils and the Party seemed inevitable. The councils were showing trends towards anarcho-syndicalism which would have resulted in the equal sharing of power in the economy between the Party and the workers. The Party had plans to introduce democratic centralism which would place all power in the hands of the Party and its designated representatives. The Polish Socialist Party (PPS) sided with the workers in this dispute and became very active in the councils and the trade unions. The local members of the PPS pushed the workers toward an egalitarian approach in the economy in order to check the growing power of the Polish Workers Party. The PPS felt that the workers were the only true counterweight to the communists.

On May 26, 1945, the Central Committee of the Party issued a

new economic reform in the name of greater efficiency and productivity. The Central Committee increased and strengthened the authority
of the plant directors and foremen. The powers of the councils were
curtailed. The director of an enterprise was to decide on all matters
related to the operation of a factory and not defer to the councils. The
councils were left with advising management on affairs related to the
level of employment in the firm and on cultural and material matters
affecting the work force. Management would have the final say in all
situations. The councils lost all control over the purse strings of the
factory and had become nothing more than a social welfare agency
for the work force.[4]

The workers did not respond well to these new moves by the
Party. Although production did increase for the rest of 1945, the
rate was not as high as had been predicted due to worker resistance.
Strikes, absenteeism, and slowdowns became constant features of the
economic scene. The councils and the PPS provided the leadership
for these protest actions. The PPS formed the core of the leadership
of the protest strikes in the Cegielski works in Poznan in August 1945.
The strike was called to protest food price increases issued that summer. When the strike was finally put down, the leadership received
prison terms for instituting illegal strike actions. Food shortages led
to strikes in other cities such as Lodz. At least a dozen strikes occurred in Lodz over a two month span. Workers' councils were again
at the forefront blaming the Party for the lack of food and more
stringent work rules. The PPS joined in on these attacks and tried
to use the councils and the trade unions to develop a stronger power
base for themselves against the Party. The Party recognized this and
continued to issue new worker controls.[5]

In late 1945, Wladyslaw Gomulka, First Secretary of the Polish
Workers Party, stated that the greatest obstacle standing in front of a
rejuvenated Polish economy was a lack of worker discipline. To correct
this problem a series of new laws were introduced the following year
in addition to reinforcing old laws. In January of 1946, a decree was
issued making work registration mandatory for all males between the
ages of eighteen and fifty-five and all women between eighteen and
forty-five with a government employment office. This process was
to insure everyone's right to work and eliminate "social parasites."
Translated, this meant that everyone had the duty to work and if one
did not do this duty, voluntarily, then the state would do it for him.
The state had the right to assign people to two years of compulsory

labor wherever it chose. Should this assignment be ignored, then the state could imprison one for five years. The threat of forced labor proved to be a useful tool against recurrent troublemakers in factories such as strike organizers. It became a widely used instrument of persecution against any independent leadership in the workers' movement.

Also expanded at this time were forced labor camps and military labor battalions, both of which were formed in 1945. One could be assigned for up to two years for lack of labor discipline. Work books and personnel passports were begun in 1946 in order to keep track of workers and cut down on illegal job shifting. These books contained the entire record of a worker including his education, military service, and, most important, his work history. Any breach of work discipline was recorded on a person's record. Once a notation was placed in a record book, it could never be removed.

Management began to take quick advantage of these new regulations by imposing heavy penalties for minor infractions of work rules. A tardy worker could be docked pay or receive a demotion after only one occurrence while after three times he could be fired thus leaving him open for assignment to compulsory labor. The councils protested these new regulations but their complaints were ignored by the government. The councils appeared neutralized. Now it was the turn of the trade unions.[6]

The reformation of trade unions began in the summer of 1944. The new unions were to be created on the basis of an individual factory or industry, not on an occupational basis. The unions and the councils were to represent the workers in the work place. According to a 1944 memorandum, the councils were to be phased out over time in favor of the unions. The Polish Workers Party was to have controlling interest in the unions with the PPS having only minor involvement. A Central Commission of Trade Unions was formed in November 1944. The Commission was made up of seventeen members of the Polish Workers Party and nine from the PPS. The chairman, secretary general, and the deputy secretary general were members of the Workers Party. The Socialists fought the monopolistic approach of the Communists. Kazimierz Witaszewski, chairman of the Trade Union Commission, voiced concern over the growing influence of the PPS in the unions and asked for greater powers to deal with this threat in 1945. Gomulka accused the Socialists of failing to cooperate with their comrades in the Party. The PPS gained steadily in local union elections because of their support for a politically free and autonomous union structure. With the incorporation of the workers' councils into the union structure in 1946, the Socialist support grew even stronger. The struggle for the leadership of the workers reached a crescendo in 1947 in Lodz.[7]

The final confrontation between the Socialist stance of egalitarianism, which seemed to be the most popular amongst the workers, and the Communist stance of democratic centralism occurred in the city of Lodz in the fall of 1947.[8]

Polish workers had become very dissatisfied and restive throughout that year. Real wages had been on a steady decline since the start of the year but dropped even faster in the summer months. Production began to lag behind proposed goals due to shortages of raw materials. As a result of these delays, work norms were not met and wages dropped drastically. To stimulate production, the authorities tried a variety of schemes. The Poznanski Works, the largest enterprise in the city, was the focus of these schemes. The authorities hoped that if their tactics worked there, a ripple effect would influence the rest of the factories in the city.

The first assault came on September 11 in the form of a plea to the patriotism of the Poznanski workers. The Trade Unions called on the workers to donate their labor on a free Saturday at their job. The profits for that day would be turned over to the authorities for the rebuilding of Warsaw. The workers were unhappy with this move since they had not been consulted about such a donation which turned out to be more of a demand than a request. The workers refused to show up for work that day. The whole incident proved an embarrassment for the Unions and showed what little influence they had on the workers.

A more forceful approach was tried next. To stimulate production, the authorities brought in work norm busters. A worker competition was initiated by the Communist Youth Union. The competition was boycotted by the workers, only one hundred workers out of six thousand took part. To compensate for the lack of local support, the authorities brought in workers from outside of the city to compete. These "new" workers were to introduce a new socialist spirit into the old work force. The workers responded with an immediate strike. Six thousand workers occupied the factory in protest against the government actions. The police were called in when the workers refused to leave the factory premises. The grounds were surrounded and the leaders of the protest were arrested. Word of the strike and the arrests spread throughout the city and sympathy strikes began to crop up in other enterprises. Within a day, forty thousand workers were idle in the city. Workers went into the streets to voice their complaints and gain sympathy from the local population. Squads of police waited for these demonstrators and clashes occurred. Some workers died in the battles with security forces but it is not known how many. The government had turned to violence just as they were to do in the future.

Resistance continued in the city despite the use of force by the government. On October 6, 1947, the authorities announced substantial increases in food stuffs in Lodz. The situation began to quiet down after this move. Top members of the Party leadership from Warsaw began to appear in the city to talk to the workers and listen to their complaints. This proved to be the last major foray by the workers before a strict Stalinist system was introduced the following year. It is important to note that precedents were set in Lodz in 1947. The workers did not strike until there was a direct assault on their standard of living and this was to be a contributing factor in the strikes of 1956, 1970, 1976, and 1980. They perceived a threat to what they had accomplished, not rising expectations over what they were to get in the future. The response of the Government to this protest was to use violence to break the will of the strikers, blame the strike on elements hostile to socialism, and finally give in to the some of the basic demands. The few gains made by the Lodz workers remained local and were to last only a short time. The authorities did not back down on their demand for increased production or their call for stricter work discipline. A strict crackdown on the workers would have to wait until a more immediate problem was taken care of: the neutralization of the Socialists who were inciting the workers.

The consolidation of power under the Polish Workers Party began to pick up speed after the summer of 1947. The Socialists had started to become restive and the lower echelons of the party were unwilling to follow the lead of the Communists. At a joint meeting of the leadership of the two parties, in July, it was decided that a purge should take place of all so-called hostile and reactionary elements in their ranks. The purge was to clear the way for the unification of the two parties. Jozef Cyrankiewicz and other leaders of the PPS carried out a rapid purge of all "rightest deviationists." The result was a rump PPS willing to be unified with the Polish Workers Party in December of 1948 to create the Polish United Workers Party (PUWP). The way was clear now to introduce a new social system; the Stalinist system.

A strict command economy was introduced into Poland in 1948. The economy was put under the control of the PUWP and guided through central planning and the system of *nomenklatura*. *Nomenklatura* is the practice of placing reliable party personnel into key positions in the economy and society in general. The economic planners became obsessed with creating heavy industry in an attempt to push Poland faster down the path toward industrialization. This mania for heavy industry production increased as the Cold War intensified in the early 1950s. Consumer goods were neglected in favor of building new towns centered around this new industry. To man these new jobs, a new work force had to be recruited. These new recruits proved to be a disruptive force amongst the old prewar working class.

The labor force grew rapidly in the late 1940s and early 1950s. The size of the working class almost doubled during this time. Many of the new laborers were peasant workers. A good portion of the industry that was introduced at this time was brought into areas where none had existed before. This was done to decrease rural unemployment and spread the number of urban workers as evenly as possible throughout the entire country. New factories were also created on the outskirts of the old industrial centers. Peasants were encouraged to apply for jobs in these new factories. The peasants looked on this employment as a way of gaining extra cash to supplement their farm income. They entered the city only to work and returned to their farms at night. They were usually found in nonmanual jobs since their skills were limited.[9]

New workers were looked on with contempt by the old working class. Anyone from the countryside was generally looked upon as being backward by those living in the city, not a situation unique to Poland. The newcomers tended to stick to their own kind and seemed confused with their new status as an urban worker. The older workers tended to view them as potential strikebreakers and the destroyers of the solidarity of the working class. The peasant-workers were generally not interested in strikes or even the workers movement, initially, since they could more easily survive economic fluctuations than their urban counterparts who had to rely on only one job to survive. Many of these peasant-workers began to move to the city after a while so that between 1950 and 1955 the urban population of Poland increased from 36 to 44 percent of the total population. The prejudices against these newcomers began to gradually decrease with time and familiarity. The peasant-workers were to add new characteristics to the workers movement, such as a traditional suspicion of power; a view that communism was a threat, not an ally; and deep religious convictions. The authorities used this split in the work force, while it existed, to further their moves towards a centrally controlled economy.[10]

The primary objective of the Polish economy, after 1947, was to increase industrial production. The authorities felt that the only way to achieve this goal was to centralize all control over production. The state became the sole employer of all workers. Since Poland was now supposed to be a proletarian state, the workers had now become owners of the factories, in theory. The workers' will was represented by the Party. Anyone opposed to the Party thus opposed the workers as well. Forms of resistance, such as strikes, became nonsense because to protest against the Party was to protest against oneself. The workers were ordered to become accomplices in their own enslavement.

All labor laws enacted since 1945 were strengthened making the manager the key figure in an enterprise. Management was given complete control over the fate of their workers. The objectives of management did not necessarily include the welfare of the workers but centered around the completion of the economic plan given to the enterprise regardless of the cost. The power of management was supported by the Trade Unions, the Party, and the security police.

Trade Unions came under strict Party control after 1949. They were organized under the Leninist principle of democratic centralism in which the Party controlled the upper echelons of the unions. They were to become "transmission belts" between the Party and the workers. Power was centered in the Central Trade Union Council which was elected by the Trade Union Congress. The process of nomenklatura was applied throughout the system even in the most basic unit of the union: the enterprise council. The principal duty of the unions was to assist management in the fulfillment of production plans by the strengthening of worker discipline. Lenin defined this function at the Soviet Trade Union Congress of 1920. The unions also had other obligations such as to raise worker efficiency, organize socialist competitions, and educate workers in the socialist ethic. There was to be no collective bargaining over wages since these were the concerns of central planning, not local interests. Protection of workers' rights, the main concern of western unions, was only of secondary importance to Polish unions. Polish worker organizations became carbon copies of their Soviet counterparts. They became an integral part of the sovietization process that was taking place in Poland at this time.

The Trade Unions voiced no protest when the work week was expanded in 1949. The forty-six hour work week was reintroduced for the general economy. This move proved to be a travesty since there already was forced overtime, mandatory attendance at political meetings, and socialist competitions. The average work week was already over fifty-two hours.

A worker's pay check was kept low by keeping production levels high and piece rates low. The wage system was based on "norms." Norms set production levels and were established at the central planning stage. The norm system became a form of compulsory labor since they were based upon conditions beyond the worker's control. Workers were forced to work long hours in order to meet their quota, which often went unmet due to frequent shortages and delays.

Workers were not permitted to leave or quit their jobs. Worker mobility between jobs became a hindrance to efficiency. Gradually, the Polish worker was tied to his job just as a medieval serf was tied to his. He was checked by Security Police for punctual arrival at work, regular attendance, and for any infraction of worker discipline. Any deviation or sign of resistance brought severe punishment.

If a worker felt cheated, he had only two options of complaint open to him. He could go to the enterprise personnel office which was generally under the direction of the Security Police or go to the Trade Union official for the factory, usually a Party official. Workers were given no outlet by which to vent their frustrations or ways to rectify the problems facing them. Continual complainers could be fired, transferred, or made persona non grata in an enterprise.

Due to the restrictions put upon society by the authorities, the most common tool used by the workers to make their position known, the strike, became virtually unheard of in the early 1950s. Two major strikes occurred during this time: one in Szczecin in the shipbuilding industry and the second in the Dabrowa mining region. Very little is known about the strikes. In both cases, the strikers were described as enemies of the people and military force was used to crush the protests. It is probable that more strikes occurred but much of this data has been lost due to the State's control of information.

Passive resistance became the key to worker protest during the

Stalinist years. Despite the use of worker passbooks, which were issued to keep a worker tied to his job, illegal job changes took place.
Shortages of skilled labor permitted some workers to move about from
job to job because management needed these people and they were
willing to bend rules to meet their planned goals and keep under
budget. Other forms of protest used by the workers were large-scale
absenteeism, disregard or evasion of orders, falsifying of records, pilfering of enterprise property to sell on the black market, the creation
of substandard goods, and the intentional destruction of machinery.
The effect of these actions was a slowdown throughout the entire economy. Each part of the Polish economy was interlinked with another
based on the central plan; should a slowdown occur in one part of the
system, it would have repercussions throughout the entire system.
The workers held in their hands a very powerful weapon only they
did not realize it. They had not learned to coordinate their activities
yet.

     The workers were to suffer greatly from the first three and six-
year plans from 1947 to 1955. Heavy industry was the prime concern
of these plans with little interest given to agricultural or consumer
goods. Great shortages of consumer products and basic commodities
became noticeable to the general public by the end of 1951. Rationing
had to be introduced in September of that year to permit some form of
equal distribution of scarce goods. This rationing was to last until the
end of 1953 when new price increases were introduced. Consumption
in Poland had increased 16.5 percent between 1948 and 1950 but it
rose only 2.8 pecent between 1951 and 1953. The real wages of Polish
workers almost doubled from 1951 to 1955 while the cost of living
more than doubled. By 1955, real wages were only half of what they
were in 1939. In 1954, an average Polish worker, with a family of
four, lived on $31.10 a month. He had to work twenty-two minutes
for a pound of wheat bread, three hours for a pound of beef, and six
and a half hours for a pound of butter. Many of these products were
not easily obtained even if the money was there. This situation led
to a very monotonous diet and a chronic wave of pilfering in order to
keep food on the table.˙ In comparison to the 25 percent decrease in
real wages for the workers, productivity increased by over 50 percent
between 1950 and 1954. The workers were not blind to this fact and
began to press their demands for change along with the rest of Polish
society as de-Stalinization began to grip the Eastern Bloc.[11]

     After the Twentieth Party Congress of the Communist Party of

the Soviet Union in 1955 and Nikita Khrushchev's anti-Stalin speech,
the Party intelligentsia in Poland began an intense campaign of criticism of the abuses of the Stalinist system. Members of the writers
union started a more general struggle for civil and political freedom.
The newspaper *Zycie Warszawy* and the weekly *Po Prostu* led the
attacks on the failings of the Stalinist bureaucrats. They took great
relish in exposing individual scandals and *apparatchik* incompetence.
Great care was taken never to criticize the socialist system, only the
Stalinist version of it. Although criticism was allowed, it had its limitations because the Party still remained in control. The workers read
the criticisms being published in the media about the Party and its
bungling of the economy. The workers were quite familiar with the
problems being printed since they had faced them every day for the
previous nine years.

The authorities knew that changes had to be made in the system.
Most of the Party members were reluctant to introduce any major
changes to the system of centralized control. To stem the growing
tide of discontent, some superficial changes were introduced and a
rudimentary dialogue between the Party and the workers was begun
in the factories. One of the earliest meetings occurred at the FSO
automobile factory in Warsaw. The meetings consisted of members
of the Party, the trade union organization, and the workers. They
met to discuss the problems facing the Polish economy and possible
solutions for them. Two major recommendations grew out of the
discussions: to set up experimental enterprises and the recreation
of workers' councils. Experimental enterprises were to try out new
techniques in management which would foster increased efficiency by
the managerial staff and the workers by allowing them to share in
the profits and the responsibilities of running a plant. The workers'
councils were to represent the workers in the everyday running of
the plant and were to have shared responsibilities with management.
The working class was to take an active part in the running of "their"
enterprise. The Party secretary of the FSO plant was quick to add
that the council's purpose was not to run the enterprise but only to
make recommendations to the directors. One can see very clearly that
the old argument that began ten years earlier had resurfaced again.
The tension between the democratic centralism of the Party and the
view of shared power by the workers was to come into the open again
soon after the events of June in 1956.[12]

The summer demonstrations of 1956 centered around the workers of the Cegielski Enterprise. The Cegileski Works was the largest enterprise in Poland employing over 15,000 people. In addition to being the largest work force in Poland, they were also amongst the highest paid. The Cegielski Works was considered a "cinderella" enterprise because of the important place it held in the new export business that the Polish government was starting. The workers played a very important role in building up the reputation and prestige of the Cegielski works, yet they felt that they were being cheated out of their just rewards and basic needs.

In general, in the city of Poznan, food supplies were poor and inconsistent and new housing was virtually nonexistent, only 29 out of 2,500 families applying for a new apartment received one. In the Cegielski Works, in particular, working conditions had deteriorated beyond safe levels. Certain sections of the factory had become unhealthy to work in, while others, due to lack of safety precautions, became downright dangerous. The spark that set off the workers' protest over these terrible conditions was the withholding of promised tax credits.

The workers found out in May of 1955 that they did not receive a promised tax rebate in their checks for that month. In their minds, they were being swindled out of a rebate that had been promised them in 1954 that amounted to 11 million zlotys. To set fuel to the growing fire, the authorities introduced new work norms that month. The increased production norms would have decreased wages by 3.5 percent. Due to bad supplies and shortages of raw materials, the norms (old or new) could not be met, hence wages would decline even further. While all this was progressing, the Party kept telling the people what a resounding success the last six-year plan had been and how the proletariat was enjoying ever soaring prosperity. The gap between the slogans of the Party and the reality of an ever decreasing standard of living became too much for the workers to bear. Faced with the very real threat of losing all they had struggled for, the workers decided to organize a mass demonstraticn to make their feelings felt.[13]

The workers initially approached the enterprise management, the local Party authorities, and their trade union representatives with their demands for change. The workers were rebuffed at every turn. Faced with no other choice, they decided to submit their demands to Warsaw, independent of all local officials. The leadership for this movement came from section W3 which built railroad cars and was made up of two thousand workers. They called for a meeting on June 23 to organize and voice their grievances. Representatives from other parts of the factory also came to discuss problems and other protest actions. The demands put forth included the payment of the promised tax rebate, an end to the new work norms, an end to the harsh work rules of the last nine years, an end to success propaganda, the beginning of an open dialogue on the real situation in Poland, the creation of authentic worker organizations free of State control, and the creation of a workers' senate in the Sejm. If these demands were ignored then strikes and public demonstrations were to be the next step.[14]

A representation of thirty workers was chosen to go to Warsaw to talk to the minister of Machine Industry. The talks took place on Tuesday, June 26, and lasted for seven hours. Of the demands presented, only the payment of the tax rebate and a slight pay increase were formally agreed upon. All other requests were left for future discussion. The workers came away from the meeting disappointed and unwilling to let their other grievances drop. The delegation split up in Warsaw, for some unknown reason, and only some returned to Poznan that night. The delegates that returned met with the workers to explain what had happened and discuss future options. A mass demonstration was to be held on Thursday morning by the Cegielski workers. It was to be a peaceful march from the factory to the city center.

People massed outside the gates of the factory early on the morning of June 28. They brought with them banners and placards that read "We want bread" and "We want lower prices and higher wages." As the Cegielski workers wound their way through the city streets, people from other factories joined the march. A prearranged work stoppage virtually shut down the entire city. The marchers remained calm except for shouting an occasional slogan. The police that lined the route talked and joked with the protesters.

Everything progressed according to plan until an unforeseen event turned the march into a riot. For some unknown reason, a group of workers seized a police car and used its loudspeaker to announce the arrest of several of the workers who had been sent to Warsaw. The crowd began to shout demands for the release of their friends. New signs began to appear in the crowd that now read "Down with communism" and "Down with the Soviets." The crowd was now told to march on the Security Police headquarters to free their friends. The crowd split with half going to the Police headquarters and half going to the city square and the Party headquarters. Along the new route, several government buildings were attacked and ransacked. When the crowd reached the city center, they demanded to speak to Premier Jozef Cyrankiewicz. The crowds were told to go home. After four hours of waiting, the people got angry and began to take matters into their own hands. The Party headquarters was sacked and several public buildings were set on fire. In the meantime, the other crowd reached the security building. The headquarters was placed under siege. As the crowd pressed forward, shots were fired from the building and several workers fell dead. A Polish flag was brought out and dipped in the blood of those killed. By midday, two lorries of soldiers and three tanks arrived to relieve the siege. Yet when the soldiers arrived, they handed over their weapons and tanks to the protesters. New security forces arrived in the late afternoon and a pitched battle ensued. Makeshift barricades were hastily constructed and Molotov cocktails were prepared, but the workers could not hold up against the attacks by tanks and helicopters. The main battle was over by the end of the day. The unofficial body count for the day was set at over 200 dead. Periodic fighting was to continue for another two days.[15]

Premier Cyrankiewicz arrived in Poznan soon after the disturbances had ended. He had come to view the damage done to the city. In a speech to the citizens of Poznan, he vowed that anyone raising his hand against the peoples power (the Party) will have it chopped off." Edward Gierek and other Politburo members came to talk to the Cegielski workers to convince them that their grievances were being addressed and that changes were soon in coming.

Workers from across the country followed the events in Poznan, as best they could, and took the promises of reform seriously. From August to October, workers' councils began to spring up spontaneously throughout the country. The factories of Warsaw became the focal point of this activity. The employees of the Zeran Autoworks was one of the first groups to form a workers' council. Other factories followed their example. Although they had no legal status, the councils began to function as if they had. They operated in the open and began to hold regular meetings. They held open discussions on reforms related to their immediate needs and to the economy at large. They organized their own factory newspapers in order to spread the news of their activities. The workers also began to print articles by dissident writers whose work had been rejected by the central office or censorship. The intelligentsia began to take part in the discussions held by the Councils. The workers actively supported the new leadership that was forming in the government under Wladyslaw Gomulka, the newly reinstated First Secretary of the PUWP. The workers really believed Gomulka when he said their was a "Polish road to socialism."

The authorities began to make concessions to the workers as early as July of 1956. The Seventh Plenary session of the Central Committee met to discuss possible reforms for the state and the economy. It was decided at the meeting that wage scales needed to be reevaluated, that a loosening of the centralized economy was needed, and that possibly the workers' councils should be reactivated, This proved to be a welcome step in the right direction but the plenum also made other resolutions that were to negate the workers' councils. They resolved that factory managers should have increased power over the local economic plan and his staff. They also increased the powers of the local union officials. The unions were given greater control over working conditions, the standard of living of the workers, the drafting of production plans, and the spending of surplus enterprise funds. These were precisely the same areas that the independent workers' councils were claiming jurisdiction over. The Party was still the arbitrator of all power.[16]

The workers disregarded the attempts by the Party to build up the prestige of the Unions. They continued to form their own councils as true representatives of workers' interests. By October of 1956, it became clear to the Party that they would have to recognize the councils or risk another outbreak of strikes and violence. Gomulka declared that:

> We must approve and welcome the initiatives of the working class regarding a better organization of industrial management and working class participation in the management of an enterprise . . . , the State must work intensely to assist the initiative of the workers.

The following month a worker's council law was passed.[17]

The bill legalizing workers' councils was passed on November 19. The law set down the basic guidelines by which a council could be formed and outlined the duties of a council. The forming of a council was made very simple. A majority vote of the workers in an enterprise was necessary to form a recognized council. Voting procedure

was left to the discretion of the members. A secret ballot was allowed
and democratic centralism need not be adhered to. The councils were
to be made up of at least two thirds manual workers. Councils could
be formed in three groups of industry; manufacturing, construction,
and agriculture. The duties of these organizations seemed varied on
the surface. The workers were given the right to assist in the for-
mulation of production plans, decide on the type of goods produced,
approve the enterprise organizational structure, discuss matters related to norms and wages, and assist the director in deciding upon
investments for the enterprise. The councils were also to approve the
appointment of a factory director. The workers were given direct responsibility for production plan fulfillment and worker discipline. In
actuality, the councils were given only an advisory position with little
or no power. All major decisions related to an enterprise were still
controlled by central planning. Work norms, wages, and quotas were
set beyond the enterprise level. The Councils were left with the duty
of cleaning up waste and increasing worker discipline. The workers
could only agree or disagree on what was handed to them. They had
no power to change the situation. If an individual council tried to
make changes in a plan, the director was given power to veto any
such move as contrary to the national plan. The principle of one-
person management was not to be hindered by the Councils. The
Party wanted the councils to be a safety valve for workers' frustrations. They had hoped that a token attempt at representation for the
workers would be enough. Some workers had other plans in mind.[18]

A majority of the workers were not pleased with the role delegated to them by the 1956 law. They viewed the councils as alternative worker representation replacing the old Party trade unions. The
Party considered the councils as an end unto themselves while the
workers saw them as a beginning. The councils began to take on duties beyond those delegated to them. Plans were made to form housing and consumer cooperatives under the direction of the councils.
The cooperatives were to be run by funds collected by the councils
and were to be interenterprise undertakings. Contact and cooperation between different councils increased greatly in 1957. Open discussions, covering a wide range of topics, were put on regularly for
the public. Political reform proved to be a very popular topic at these
meetings. The authorities were becoming quite concerned over these
activities because they had no control over them. By 1958, the government decided that it was time to stop talking and get back down

to work.[19]

The Party launched a two prong attack in 1957 and 1958 in an attempt to bring the workers back under their control. The first phase was to revive the official trade unions, and secondly, subjugate the growing self-management (*samorzad*) movement in the workers' councils. The old trade union structure was preserved and the concept of democratic centralism was enhanced. The old Stalinist, KIosiewicz, was replaced as head of the trade union council by a loyal follower of Gomulka, Ignacy Loga-Siwinski. Attempts were made to improve the outward appearance of the Unions but underneath it all they were still controlled by the Party. According to the Trade Union press, the union was to defend the interests of the working class by combining their defense with increasing production. It was the same old package with new wrappings. New laws were passed that increased the powers of the shop committees in order to make them more responsive to the needs and demands of the workers. The ninth plenum of the central committee of the Party decided that the trade Unions would assume the policy-making functions of the workers' councils as soon as possible. It was also decided that the enterprise directors veto power should be expanded to have more control over the Councils.[20]

Despite the changes made in the trade union organization, the workers still looked on them with disdain, referring to them as the "second government." The workers saw them as nothing more than a clique supporting the bureaucratic management. The unions were even attacked in *Po Prostu* and *Nowe Drogi* as having lost the respect and trust of the workers.

Regardless of the workers response, the die had been cast by the Party. The creation of overlapping duties for the Trade Unions and the Councils gave the Party the excuse it needed to reorganize the enterprise structure to create a more efficient system. Four bases of power had evolved in factories: the workers' councils, the director, the Trade Union, and the Party. Authority had become blurred and it needed to be clarified. The solution to the problem was the creation of the Conference for Workers Self Government.

The Conference for Workers Self Government, known as the KSR, was in theory to become a labor parliament. The law organizing the KSR was passed on December 20, 1958. The four main power bases of the enterprise were to be given equal representation of one vote each. The workers' councils would always be out-voted by three to one since the director, the Trade Union, and the Party were all allies. The KSR was given five basic responsibilities; to raise the economic level of the enterprise, to strengthen worker discipline, increase production, watch over worker safety, and educate the worker in the socialist ethic. The KSR was given the right to "examine" and "evaluate" other operations in the enterprise but was given no power beyond advisory. At the second annual conference, held in 1959, it was decided that the major task of the workers' councils was to be worker mobilization and discipline. The Councils had become nothing more than extensions of the enterprise administration. By 1962, *Trybune Ludu*, the organ of the Central Committee, argued that there was no longer any need to worry about the KSR because 60 to 70 percent of its members were Party members.[21]

The response to the destruction of the Councils was apathy. The workers found themselves alone in defense of their rights. The intelligentsia went their own way virtually ignoring the workers by the early 1960s. The Catholic Church, which would become a very active ally of the workers, was not in a position to apply any pressure on the government since it was going through a rebuilding process after the Stalinist period. The Church and the intelligentsia were to become active allies of the workers movement in the 1970s and 1980s. The workers movement was to go into a period of dormancy in Poland until 1970. The 1960s proved to be a period of stagnation for the Polish worker but by the end of the decade it was becoming obvious that decline was setting in and something had to be done to stop it. The government's solution was announced in late 1970 and the worker's response came in the Baltic port of Gdansk on December 12, 1970.

Chapter Two

We Are Workers Not Hooligans

Worker unrest, in Gdansk in 1970, began when the state planning commission introduced new wage guidelines for 1971. The new regulations set higher production goals and higher piece rates which would have virtually eliminated bonuses and decreased wages but would have increased the average work load for production workers. These changes came after a prolonged period of stagnation in workers' living standards. Many workers relied on their monthly bonus to make ends meet and without this added income their standard of living would have declined drastically. The new wage regulations were to be introduced over a period of time and through an intricate process which few people could understand. Workers from all over the country filed complaints over this new plan with the greatest number of letters coming from Gdansk. Stanislaw Kociolek, a vice premier, politburo member, and former Gdansk Party secretary, was sent to Gdansk to answer the workers' questions in regard to the economic changes. He arrived two days before the strikes in the city began.

The majority of the workers on the seacoast were young, rural immigrants working in what had become the new cinderella industry of the Polish economy: shipbuilding. Of the 16,000 workers in the Lenin shipyards, 3,000 of them still lived in the factory hostels. In Gdansk there was a working class that was socially compact and overwhelmingly employed in one industry. The workers of this city also had extensive contact with the outside world, because of the tourist trade in this Baltic region.

Stanislaw Kociolek arrived for talks with the workers in Gdansk on December 12, 1970. Kociolek had been sent to try to explain to the workers the new economic changes that were to be introduced within the next few weeks. The workers tried to negotiate changes in the plan in order to decrease the severity of its impact on them and their families lives. The vice premier told them that no changes could be made in the plan and also informed them that consumer price changes would be introduced in two days. The workers were told that they would have to work harder for less pay and less food. The men at the shipyard did not feel consoled and did not leave the yards after the meeting. Approximately 3,000 workers stayed in the shipyards and began to hold ad hoc meetings to discuss the pay changes and the price changes. A strike was called in the shipyards for 5 o'clock that afternoon. They were soon joined by the dockers of the city. Word of the strike spread quickly throughout the region and sympathy strikes were called in Gdynia and Sopot, sister cities of Gdansk. Meetings lasted into the night and the next day. The authorities responded to the strikes by sealing off the city from the rest of the country. A number of arrests were made of anyone suspected of influencing the workers.

After two days of discussions, the strikers drew up a petition requesting that the authorities stop the loading of Polish ships in the port with food for export and to divert this food to the home market. Two delegations were sent with the petition to the regional Party headquarters. Neither delegation returned to the Yard. Fearing for the safety of the men they sent to represent them, the shipyard workers left the Yard and converged on the Party buildings to find out the fate of their colleagues. The workers picked up more people as they marched along. The protestors split into three groups; one group went on to the Party headquarters, a second group went to the Gdansk Polytechnic Institute, and the third went to a radio station in the suburb of Wrzeszcz. The students refused to lend aid to the demonstrators and remained in their dormitories. The third group tried to persuade the radio operators to join the protest and allow them to broadcast strike reports to the rest of the country. The radio personnel refused to cooperate. These attempts to spread the newly started revolt failed miserably.

The first group of strikers reached the Party headquarters by afternoon and demanded that the local Party secretary come out to speak to them. At first no response was given and the crowd began to chant "Bread!" and the "Press lies." Finally a minor official, Stanislaw Jundzill, was sent out to address the crowd but he was greeted with whistles and jeers. He returned to the building and then nothing was heard from the building for some time. The silence was finally broken by the building's loudspeakers announcing that there would be no negotiations conducted with a mob. The workers were told to return to their jobs and act like responsible citizens. The security militia at this point filed out of the building and formed a cordon around it. The crowd was furious and began to press the militia to get into the building. The security forces responded to this pressure with truncheons and clubs. Open fighting erupted between the police and the crowd. The fighting spread into the city where looting and burning of shops took place. Over sixty shops were destroyed during seven hours of violence.[1]

Tensions were still running high the next day. The workers did not return to their jobs but instead held demonstrations in front of the regional Party headquarters, the district police building, and the municipal government building. Still angry from the previous day's encounter with the Party, the crowd erupted and charged the Party stronghold. The militia was caught off guard and the protestors took the building. Some Party members were forced to surrender under a flag of truce while others were lifted from the roof by helicopter. Once the structure was evacuated it was set on fire. The crowd now moved on to the police headquarters to free those arrested the day before. Police fired automatic weapons into the throngs of people. An unknown number of people were killed and wounded but the crowd pressed on and took the building. It too was set afire and several policemen were hung from nearby street lamps. The crowd now went on a burning spree setting fire to two more groups of buildings and a Russian merchant ship at dock in the harbor. A curfew was ordered for the city but rioting persisted into the night. Kociolek went on local television that evening to urge the workers to return to their jobs. That same evening, Zenon Kliszko, a confidant of Gomulka, arrived in the city with special detachments of riot police.[2]

On Wednesday, December 16, the workers returned to the Lenin Shipyards but not to work. They met and decided to march again into the city but this time the situation proved to be different. When they tried to leave the yards, they were stopped by tanks and armored cars. The security police had surrounded the shipyards and refused anyone passage in or out. A group of workers tried to force their way out and the militia opened fire into the crowd. Two men were killed and eleven were wounded. The remainder of the crowd retreated back into the yards. It was here that the tactics of the striking workers changed from open confrontation to holding hostage the means of production. An occupation strike was called and strike committees were elected. These committees drew up lists of formal demands that included pay raises, a reduction in taxes, a price freeze on essential consumer products, withdrawal of the army and the militia from the city, and punishment for those responsible for the state of the economy. The workers refused to return to work until their demands were met by high level government officials. The dock workers and the Gdansk Repair Shipyards joined the strike but did not coordinate their activities with the Lenin Yards. Workers from nearby Gdynia tried to join the activities in Gdansk but they found that the city had been sealed off by army roadblocks and that all telephone lines into the area had been severed. That evening, Kociolek again went on local television to persuade the workers to return to their jobs and resume "normal work."[3]

The strike still continued in Gdansk on Thursday when word of the massacre in Gdynia arrived. A large number of workers heeded the vice premier's request and decided to return to work at the Gdynia shipyards that morning. As the workers of the first shift dismounted their buses and approached the yard gates they were attacked. The militia had set up a crossfire, to protect the yards from hooligans. The workers were caught unprotected. Tanks and helicopters were brought in to assist in militia. When the chaos ended, according to unofficial sources, over three hundred people had been killed or wounded.[4]

The news of the Gdynia massacre appears to have had an adverse effect on the strikers in Gdansk. After the news reached them, the strike committees began to search for a way to end their strike quickly but still receive some concessions. The police made the first move by releasing some of the workers arrested during the riots. The authorities also agreed to open talks on the strikers' demands. The dockworkers were the first to return to work while the shipyard held out for three more days. By December 23, Radio Gdansk reported that the curfew had been lifted and that most workers had returned to their jobs. Edward Gierek, the new Party first secretary, sent a letter to the workers of the city "expressing his thanks for the immediate resumption of work." In his Christmas homily, Cardinal Wyszynski called for forgiveness and compassion. A temporary calm settled over the city while news of a strike in the port city of Szczecin began to slowly filter in.[5]

The first news of the Gdansk riots reached Szczecin on December 16. The S.S. *Slupsk*, a freighter, had been diverted from Gdansk due to the serious conditions there. While the ship was being unloaded, the sailors from the ship talked with some of the dock workers and shipyard workers and described the situation in Gdansk as they saw it before leaving the harbor. The workers decided to call a sympathy strike for the next day.

Strike committees at the Warski Shipyards were quickly formed and the authorities were approached to open talks on the state of the economy and the events in Gdansk and Gdynia. The factory management, the local Party organization, and the trade unions refused to recognize the existence of the strike committees. The workers were quite angered over this lack of recognition and decided to carry their protest directly to the local Party headquarters. Workers from other factories and people from off the street joined the protest march. People in the crowd began to shout "Gomulka out!" as well as other slogans. Party representatives refused to talk to the crowd. The workers had reached an unbearable level of frustration. Representatives of the workers were refusing to recognize the existence of the workers or the problems that faced them. To vent their frustrations, the protestors set the building on fire. Security forces began to fire into the crowd as the building began to burn. The confrontation between the security militia and the people lasted for hours. The regional Party leaders had to be evacuated from the city in armored cars. As the day progressed, the crisis in the city grew worse. The police and the security headquarters were burnt to the ground. Looting and fires broke out in the shopping district. Frantic appeals were broadcast over the radio for people to stay home and keep their children inside. Workers were urged to stand guard in defense of the socialist system. A strict curfew was put into force that night but fighting still persisted. That evening, an interfactory strike committee was formed at the Warski Shipyards. The Committee called a general strike for Szczecin. Within two days, the strike committee was in complete control of the entire city. The army and the security forces were forced to negotiate with the workers' strike committee to maintain order in the city. The streets were now patrolled by the strikers' militia. Signs began to appear throughout the city that read "This is an economic strike not a political one." and "We are workers not hooligans." The workers began to publish their own newspapers and broadcast their own radio programs. They were determined to make sure that the people heard the truth of the events in Szczecin. These activities were to provide invaluable experience for the strikes of 1980. Open elections were also held for the workers' councils. The elections were conducted by secret ballot and open to anyone. Edmund Baluka, a member of the interfactory strike committee and a well known local labor activist, was elected to the Warski council at this time. Baluka was to become the chief spokesman for the workers in Szczecin. The general strike in the city lasted until December 22. Strikes were to spread to Slupsk, Krakow, Nowa Huta, Elblag, and Warsaw. By Christmas, the situation in Poland had quieted but this peace was to be shortlived.[6]

On January 2, 1971, the Lenin Shipyards were again on strike. The workers were demanding the release of 200 workers still held by police and the appearance of Gierek at the yards to hear their complaints. The strike was led by the strike committees that were formed in December but had now changed their names to worker committees. The change of name to worker committees suggests that they intended to remain active after the strike was over. Membership in these committees was decided by election and two of the people elected to them were Anna Walentynowicz and Lech Walesa. The first order of business for these new worker representatives was to draw up a new list of demands and present them to the management of the shipyards. The demands went beyond the economic realm and included the release of all demonstrators arrested during the strike and a moratorium on further sanctions against the workers, punishment for those responsible for the murders in Gdansk and Gdynia, the improvement of public information, the transformation of trade unions into true representatives of the workers, and the free election of local union officials. Two managers from the Yards were sent to Warsaw to discuss and report on these new demands. Stanislaw Kociolek was sent back to Gdansk to talk to the strikers. The workers were outraged that the man they blamed for the massacres of December had been sent to talk to them. Another demand was quickly added to their list, the dismissal of Kociolek from the government. The government refused to take any other actions when the workers refused to talk to Kociolek. A general strike was called for January 18 to protest this latest government move. The strike demands were again submitted to management. The shipyard manager agreed to meet all economic demands but refused to discuss any of the other requests. Most of the workers accepted this response and returned to work the next day. The other demands were not forgotten and were resubmitted on January 19.[7]

In an attempt to split the workers' movement, Gierek met with handpicked representatives of the dockworkers and the Gdansk Repair Shipyards. These "worker" representatives not only included workers but also foremen, a director, and a department head. These representatives gave Gierek pledges of loyalty, on behalf of the other workers of the region, and promised to increase production. Gierek thanked them for their pledges and stated that "one can examine and solve all problems in a thoughtful way, in an atmosphere of calm, order, and thorough work." The Lenin Shipyard workers were not asked to any of these meetings. The workers that met with Gierek were branded as traitors on their return home. They were called fools because Gierek had accepted their work pledges but gave nothing in return. This poor attempt to manufacture worker support for the new government backfired and angered the workers even more. The workers increased their demands so that up to 2,000 a day were being submitted to regional Party headquarters by January 22. It was finally decided that Gierek should meet with the workers.[8]

The situation in Szczecin paralleled that of Gdansk so that by mid-January this city was also on strike. A general strike was called for Sunday, January 23, for the entire city of Szczecin by the workers' committees. The strike again closed down the city for the second time in less than a month. A new interfactory strike committee was elected with Edmund Baluka at its head. The committee took over maintenance of the city and the distribution of food. The old demands were resubmitted with one emphasized in particular; a face to face meeting with the new Party general secretary, Gierek.

The following day, Edward Gierek and members of his new government, including the minister of defense Wojciech Jaruzelski, arrived in Szczecin. When Gierek arrived at the Warski Yards he had to ask the permission of the inter-factory strike committee to enter the grounds. He then had to walk to the meeting hall through the mass of strikers. The worker delegates were already waiting for him in the hall. The delegates were elected by secret ballot to represent each section. Of the eighty three delegates elected to meet with Gierek, 40 percent were Party members. Since the vote was open and secret, this shows that some of the workers had respect for some of the rank and file of the Party. The meeting lasted for nine hours and was broadcast in the shipyards over loudspeakers.

Baluka greeted the guests of the strikers at the hall door and then led them to the rostrum. When Gierek and his entourage were all seated, Baluka then read them the workers' demands, the same demands that had been put forth in December, in Szczecin and Gdansk. After the demands were read, Gierek spoke to the workers in the hall and in the yards. He asked the workers for patience in solving the economic problems of the nation. He told the workers that "the only solution is that you work still harder so that our economy produces its maximum." Once Gierek ended his speech, the floor was opened to questions and opinions. Many of the comments and questions centered around working conditions and the deaths of the workers in December. At the end of the meeting one delegate took the microphone to give a warning to the authorities, "If in a year or two there is no improvement then we will say: Comrades we were deceived." He left the possibilities of what this deception might lead to open to speculation. From Szczecin, Gierek went to meet the workers in Gdansk.[9]

The First Secretary arrived in Gdansk on January 25. He first met with the local Party leaders and the directors of the shipping industry in the region and from there went on to the Lenin Shipyards. It was there that Gierek had his first contact with the strikers of Gdansk. An open debate ensued for several hours about the economy and the events of December. The workers were satisfied with the talks and the promises of change. At the end of the meeting Gierek addressed the workers telling them that only hard work and diligence would overcome the obstacles facing the Polish economy. He ended the speech with the question "Will you help us?" The workers were to have responded "We will!" The workers returned to their jobs the next day.[10]

The new government worked quickly in getting a new economic program started especially after the meetings on the seacoast and another strike in Lodz in February. Gierek's Great Leap Forward, as it was called, was launched at the 8th Plenum of the Central Committee of the Party and was to be Poland's second industrial revolution. The plan called for the consolidation and centralization of political power by the Party, as instruments in the implementation of the new economic push forward. Since political power was already in the hands of the Party, Gierek was actually calling for more power. To carry out these reforms, Western credits were to be used as a temporary crutch to support the new system. The money would be used to update the old enterprises and create new ones. The enterprises of Poland would also be reorganized into new industrial complexes, called WOGs. The

WOGs were organized for greater economic coordination and easier control. By 1975, the WOGs were under the control of a Central Committee staff. These new complexes were groups of factories that were joined together from the same branch of industry for greater efficiency. By 1975, 67 percent of all Polish industrial output was controlled by WOGs. This new system called for greater centralized control and gave greater control over the workers to management. One of the objectives of the WOGs was to create greater profits. Management's responsibilities for the creation of this new profit was even greater than before. Although new responsibilities and powers were relegated to management, they still had the same shortages and bottlenecks to deal with that they had before. To make sure only reliable Party personnel were in managerial positions, the *nomenklatura* list was expanded. Heavy industry was again emphasized to the neglect of consumer goods, health care, and housing. Many of the basic consumer products that were used by the Polish people had to be bought abroad with Western credits. It was not until 1976 that attention was turned to light consumer industry.

Gierek not only bought consumer goods abroad with Western credits but also increased the workers wages with the same money. He tried to buy legitimacy for his new government with better wages and more Western consumer goods. Wages were to increase by over 40 percent in the first five years of Gierek's rule. The authorities had hoped that by doing this the workers would forget about the promises made back in January to increase worker democracy. The authorities had no intention of sharing power with the workers. Gierek made vague promises of increasing interunion democracy and improving the image of the unions. This proved to be illusory because a new government ministry was created to take over many of the unions' responsibilities. The ministry of labor, wages, and social affairs took away the trade unions' remaining powers over employment, wages, and work conditions. While Gierek talked of giving more freedom, the government gained more control over the economy than they had had since the Stalinist days.[11]

Despite the authorities' attempts to buy off the workers with greater pay and more items to buy, the workers were tired of being taken for granted and wanted a say over the path of their lives. The workers no longer wanted to depend on an impersonal autocratic bureaucracy. After 1970, the workers gained some self confidence and boasted that "now we know how to push them back." They began to regard certain rights as inalienable such as unconditional security of employment, relatively light labor discipline, and a steadily rising standard of living. Despite the basic demands placed by the workers in 1970–71, one of the most pushed for demands was for revitalized workers councils. In a public opinion poll held by *Rada Robotnicza*, the overwhelming majority of the respondents called for stronger workers councils as an independent voice for the workers and as a check on an enterprise director's powers. The same poll called for economic reforms which would give the councils more power. In another poll conducted between 1972 and 1974, the majority of higher paid and skilled workers opted for increased collective actions and these actions could be coordinated through the workers' councils. Already in Feburary of 1971, the workers took it upon themselves to form independent worker institutions. A workers conference was held in Szczecin to discuss the possibility of creating either autonomous worker's councils or trade unions. Delegates were sent to Gdynia and Gdansk to find out if the shipyard workers there would be interested in joining them. Discussions went on for several months but they folded due to an eventual lack of interest. They already had the worker committees formed in January and had promises from the authorities of a revitalized trade union system. The workers had hoped that the old system would reform itself. The majority of the workers also saw no chance of forming an independent organization on their own separate from the Party. The workers had held free elections in 1971 to worker organizations and had placed some independent people in positions of local and regional authority. It was hoped the these people would instigate reforms from below. Within a year the Party authorities began to quietly remove these "troublemakers" from their jobs by transferring them to other jobs scattered throughout the country. Through these job transfers, the leadership of the worker's councils was decimated by 1972. The majority of the workers had falsely hoped that the authorities would share power and that the Party truly wanted to reform the system. Gierek's approach was not to decentralize the power structure but to consolidate it even further than it had before. Gierek was more than willing to alleviate some of the workers material wants but ignored their demands for true representation and self expression. The initial dialogue that started between the Party and the workers began to fade quickly by 1972. The workers did not sit back quietly and accept an intolerable situation that was being reimposed on them.[12]

Labor productivity was increased initially under the Gierek plan through new contracts, bonuses, and incentive plans. Real wages grew over the first four years by 7.2 percent while productivity increased by 7.5 percent. With this increase in incentives, worker earnings became very dependent upon management discretion and performance. The managers' charter of 1972 increased their powers well beyond any that they had had before. This was also a new generation of managers who were better educated, especially in an authoritarian managerial style, and were separated from the work force because they had not risen from the shop floor. The managers increasingly began to look on their employees as objects that had to be manipulated in order to meet the plan. The younger generation of workers resented this approach. They had rioted just a few months earlier demanding greater control over the factors that influenced their income and work environment. Many disputes arose over wages and bonuses between workers and management. With the decline of the worker's councils, the workers had little choice but to turn to the "new" unions who were now more responsive, according to the government, to the workers' problems. Already in February of 1971, the trade unions faced the task of improving their image.

Glos Pracy heralded the twenty-first plenary session of the trade union central committee as the beginning of a new era of understanding and frankness between the Party and the workers. The trade unions were again given the task of forming new links between the Party and the masses. They were to become brand new transmission belts. The local unions were ordered to take the initiative in solving workers' problems rather than waiting to be prodded from above. Very few union representatives took these orders as legitimate. The representatives from Gdansk, Gdynia, Szczecin, and the Zeran Motor Works of Warsaw led the movement for real reform in the union structure including recognizing the right to strike based on legitimate grievances. They formed commissions aimed at decreasing the powers of management and the security forces in the factories. The commissions led to no significant changes. All major union reforms were postponed until the new WOGs were functioning properly. It was decided, though, that a draft of a new labor law would be started in order to update the old one dating back to the 1950s. Gierek addressed the full session of the trade union meeting on its final day of deliberation. He made it quite clear how independent these new revised unions would be when he stated that "the Party will not permit the trade unions to move away from itself." The Plenary meeting ended with the statement: "What was needed now was energetic, creative, and constructive work by factory workers." On March 2, Radio Szczecin reported that the final declaration of worker support for the Party line and resolutions of the plenary session were not well received by the workers of the region. The session was described as vague and paying little attention to the problems of the workers. This was only the beginning of the resurfacing of worker discontent.[13]

The twenty-fourth trade union congress was held in January of 1972. The Party officially reasserted its leading role of the unions at this meeting. The delegates to the congress called for improved work regulations, increased accident benefits, and extended maternity leaves. Little or no mention was made of the workers right to veto, worker self management, or institutional reform. Some delegates did bring up these points but were rebuked by Waclaw Kruczek, the new trade union chairman, for presenting demands beyond the duties of a trade union. He told them that "the government must act as the government and the trade unions as trade unions," the leading role of the Party in union affairs was to be preserved. Gierek warned the Congress that "differences" of view would not be permitted to turn into conflicts. The Congress formally recognized the leading role of the Party in its final declaration. In just over one year, the trade unions had fallen back on their old habits of following the lead of the party without question.[14]

In a poll taken in 1972, four out of every five workers questioned were dissatisfied with trade union performance since 1971. Some of the workers began to fall back on their old ways of influencing managerial decisions. The two most popular forms of protest were adjusting their work pace and illegal job changes. The work pace of an entire enterprise could be affected by frequent absenteeism and labor slow downs. The importance of plan completion under the new system was more crucial now than it had been before because one's pay was tied directly to overall output for the enterprise. Illegal job changes had the same negative effect of throwing snags into the system but not changing the system. These protests, either individual or group, gave only short-term relief to the workers' problems. The raise or new job may have benefitted them at first but had negative effects on the economy at large causing inflation and delays in output. These actions, although popular, provided no structural solutions to the problems facing the Polish economy.[15]

Strikes became a frequent feature of the Polish economic scene from 1973 to 1976. The strikes that took place were usually short in duration and involved local matters such as unpaid bonuses or food shortages. These strikes were uncoordinated actions that occurred throughout the country. The largest strike took place in the twin cities of Gdansk and Gdynia in August of 1974. The work norms were introduced in the shipyards and at the docks without prior consultation with the workers. According to the new work norms, bonuses which made up 40 to 60 percent of a basic paycheck were to be cut by 7 to 15 percent. The size of the pay cut was left to the discretion of management. The new pay regulations were introduced in the region stating that any infringement of work discipline or arbitrary disruption of work could result in the loss of one's bonus or job. The workers did not feel threatened by this new regulation and a general strike was called for the yards and docks in both cities. The army was callled in to unload ships that were backed up in the harbor. Gierek made a surprise "routine" visit to Gdansk to talk to the workers and listen to their problems. He had hoped to reenact his success of 1971, but to no avail. The workers demanded the removal of the new work norms, an end to forced work on Sundays, and the withdrawal of the Citizen's Militia (ORMO) from the yards and the docks. Gierek left promising only to look into the matter. The strikes in the region lasted until October 1 when Szczecin workers joined the protest. The next day *Glos Wybrzeza* reported that the new norm system had been withdrawn in order to consult with the workers. This tactical withdrawal by the Party did not satisfy the majority of the workers. Strikes and slowdowns continued on the seacoast into 1975. Gierek was to make three more trips to the port cities between April and September 1975. The First Secretary tried to explain to the workers that their expectations were running too high and that their standard of living was actually rising according to official-statistics. The workers told him that they did not believe the official statistics. The meetings were described as "difficult."[16]

A new labor law was introduced in 1975 in an attempt to quell the growing worker protests. The old labor code was based on laws that were passed mainly in the early 1950s. According to *Glos Pracy*, the objective of the new code was to stimulate good and honest work and to increase the workers' concerns for their enterprise and the community at large. The "new code" for the most part was a repetition of previous legislation but made great strides in enhancing the powers of a centralized management and Party and decreasing the powers of local labor organizations.

Labor contracts were now to be centrally negotiated and signed by the head offices of the branch trade unions and the minister or head of a central industrial office. The Party was to be directly involved in the negotiating process. The trade union role as a conveyor belt was reconfirmed.

The manager was to remain solely responsible for all enterprise matters. The workers' councils were given the right to submit suggestions on improving worker output in plants as well as supervising the fulfillment of enterprise plans. In the final analysis, the manager and the manager alone was responsible for the correct operation of an enterprise. Interference by a labor organization in the operation of a factory or enterprise would not be tolerated.

New forms of labor punishment were introduced in order to tighten worker discipline and stabilize the work force. The new regulations were aimed at ending illegal job shifts and excessive absenteeism. The amount of vacation time and a worker's bonus were now tied to the length of employment in the same enterprise and a worker's consistent performance there in.

Rewards were to be given to workers who showed initiative and raised productivity while penalties were increased for those who disregarded regulations and slowed progress. Decisions over rewards or punishments were left to the discretion of management.

Work reference books were reintroduced as a way of keeping data on individual workers. Management was required to keep these books up to date. The reference books were patterned after the work books of the 1950s. The books were to be made out at the cessation of employment and were to contain such data as length of service, type of work, job position, wage, skills, and reason for termination. The reference book had to be carried from job to job and also contained private assessments of the worker by management and the security forces of the plant. According to Kultura these books would not harm honest, hardworking people, just wise guys, lay-abouts, and drunkards.

The new labor code appeared to be directly targeted at those workers who were creating dissension and those thinking about it. It was an attempt by the Party to regain control over an increasingly rebellious working force.[17]

From 1971 to 1974, the percentage of state employed workers

steadily increased so that by 1975 the Party had a virtual monopoly over society through the control of wages, consumer pricing, and product supply. The promised improvements in education, health care, and housing never came about. Conditions deteriorated in these sectors. Health and education were considered nonproductive sectors of the economy so investments of capital were minimal. Housing construction fell behind schedule due to a greater demand by an ever-growing urban population. City populations were growing due to a policy of farmland confiscation by the state which forced many people to leave the countryside. The average waiting period for a new apartment was extended to ten years or more from the time a request was filed. The majority of Polish citizens were faced with these problems not just the workers. A growing number of people were isolated from these shortages and shortcomings of the Polish economy. These people were of a new privledged class that had existed since 1945 but had expanded greatly under Gierek. A list of "perks" and privileges evolved around the nomenklatura system which was expanded under the new economic reforms to show the extent of the Party's power. Managers, techno-bureaucrats, and security forces were insulated from the shortages and problems that the average worker had to face every day. They had access to special shops, which carried hard to get western goods as well as local items, access to better schools, and they found shorter waiting lists for housing. Wages of the average worker and administrative personnel grew further and further apart. The gap between the lowest and the highest paid workers in an enterprise increased by two and a half times over the five year period. This growing privileged class became more and more obvious as the decade went on and their share of the profits increased.[18]

A blatant policy of sovietization was introduced between 1975 and 1976. Attempts were made to change the Polish constitution to pattern it after the constitutions of other "People's" democracies. The leading role of the Party was to be confirmed as well as the fraternal bond between the Soviet Union and Poland. The proposed constitution stated that a citizen's rights were dependent upon one's duty to the state. The alterations to the constitution were fought by the Catholic Church, the majority of the intelligentsia, and most of the workers. The initial proposals were dropped by the authorities due to the pressure put upon them by society. Minor constitutional changes were introduced in late 1975. The Polish people also became aware of two other programs aimed at bringing Poland farther into the Soviet orbit. One program called for the confiscation of "unproductive" farm land which would be added to the state farms. To many this looked like the beginning of another attempt at the collectization of Polish agriculture. A side effect of this program was a decline in food production. The second program created a new youth organization which was to take the place of all other youth groups. The Polish Socialist Youth Union was patterned after the Soviet youth organization Komsomol and resembled the Stalinist Association of Polish Youth of the 1950s. The result of these activities was that various social groups in Polish society began to grow closer together in attempts to stop the Party in their maneuvers to bring Poland closer to the Soviet Union. The Party itself provided the tinder and the spark which were to bring the various groups formally together in the summer of 1976.[19]

The wage increases that were introduced over five years were substantial but coupled with an insufficient or unreliable supply of durable goods to spend it on meant that there was a lot of money in circulation.Much of this surplus money was spent on food. The food markets could not keep up due to a decline in food production which was a result of the state agricultural policies. To decrease the flow of excess money and to cut the growing demand for food products, the Party decided to increase food prices. The increase in food prices was a sound economic move but a poor political one. The first warning of price changes came in December of 1975 when Gierek announced that the price structure for food products was to be studied and proposals for changes submitted in 1976. No changes were to be submitted before consulting with the working people. In March, Prime Minister Piotr Jaroszewicz warned that changes in basic food prices were imminent. On June 22 and 23, top Party officials from throughout the country were 'consulted" on the price changes. The changes in food prices were introduced to the nation the next day. Food prices were to rise from 30 to 100 percent with an average increase of 69 percent. Wage increases were also announced that ranged from 280 zlotys to 600 zlotys. Members of the nomenklatura were to receive higher wages in the form of bonuses, this was not announced publicly. Strikes were called throughout the country.[20]

The response of the majority of the workers was swift and antagonistic to the price and wage changes introduced by the state. Spontaneous strikes were called throughout the country. The shipyards in Gdansk and Gdynia called general strikes. Strike committees were formed from the leadership that remained from the 1970 strike. The committee controlled the gates to the yards and refused to allow potential troublemakers participation in the sit in strike. The workers occupied the yards rather than protest in the streets. They remembered that it was safer and more productive to hold the means of production hostage than to enter the streets and be at the mercy of the security militia. The destruction and rioting that were to be the distinguishing factors of Poznan in 1956 and the events of 1970 were missing in Gdansk and Gdynia in 1976. This form of protest was also carried on in Lodz, Szczecin, Warsaw, and eventually 130 factories. The strike committees kept in contact with each other in an attempt to coordinate their activities. This form of protest based upon a determined well disciplined work force that refused to produce until its demands were met surprised the authorities and forced them to reconsider their imposition of price changes.

While the majority of the workers began to adopt the coordinated sit in strike as a form of protest, there were some who still clung to the old methods of street demonstrations. The workers in the cities of Radom, Ursus, and Plock took to the streets to make their protests known. In Ursus, 90 percent of the work force went on strike. Rioting broke out in the demonstrations just as they had in 1956 and 1970. Buildings were set on fire, property was destroyed, and shops were looted. The security militia was brought in to disperse the demonstrators with water hoses and tear gas. The strikes proved to be more flash than substance. The greatest impact of these strikes came after the Party decided to withdraw the price changes. The peaceful strikes had already forced the price withdrawals but the mistreatment of the strike leadership and the strikers in Radom and Ursus by the authorities was to be a rallying point for the intelligentsia, the Church, and the workers.[21]

Chapter Three

Three Together Make Revolution

The four year span, from the summer of 1976 to the summer of 1980, proved to be a very eventful period in Polish history. Two of the most obvious events of this period, that did much to bolster Polish national pride, were the sending of the first Polish cosmonaut into space and secondly, even more important than a Pole in space, the selection of a Pope from Poland. The election of a Polish Pope far outstripped merely mortal accomplishments and seemed to vindicate, in the minds of many Poles, their long history of suffering. The return of Pope John Paul II to his homeland proved to be a spiritual awakening for many Poles, believers and nonbelievers alike. While these events went beyond the borders of Poland proper there were others that were taking place that were to have as great an effect on the Polish people as the return of the Pope to Poland or the return of a man from space.

Following the events of June 1976, workers were arrested, beaten, and fired from their jobs by the authorities. The punishments given out to the protesters went beyond the scope of the law. Support for those who were persecuted came from fellow workers and from two other sources; one natural and one unexpected. The Catholic Church gave material and, more importantly, spiritual support to the persecuted worker activists. The intelligentsia joined the church in their support of the protestors. The formation of the Workers' Defense Committee (KOR), by intellectuals, workers, and clergy, proved only to be the beginning of a movement toward the creation of an independent society. The human rights movements melded with the free trade union movements to form a united front against the growing powers of the state authorities. It was during these four years that the leadership cadre for the strikes of 1980 was created. A new determination was developing among some of the workers to expand their demands beyond short range goals in order to make a more permanent impact on the system. The whole process was to begin in the summer of 1976. The initial spark for the June events was, again, a drastic and impromptu set of food price increases. The increases averaged 69 percent and covered all the basic foodstuffs. The price changes were coupled with a piece rate reevaluation which meant a reduction in wages. The people voiced their resentment of the changes, and not having been consulted about them, by staging sitdown strikes and to a lesser degree street protests. The major street protests were to take place in the cities of Radom and Ursus. The protests started out peacefully and turned violent after picking up people along the march route. There is speculation that instigators were planted in the crowd to spark the violence. The end result of this explosion was burnt buildings and damaged work places. Ursus workers destroyed the major railway link between the Soviet Union and East Germany as well as other railway equipment. The workers there shouted "We strike on behalf of those who cannot." In Radom, strikers marched from their work places to the local Party headquarters. The marchers were supplemented with housewives and others along the route. The building was empty but the crowd was not satisfied. The protestors went to the apartments of the Party leaders. The women entered the apartments and found them well stocked with food and modern furniture and appliances. The protestors did nothing to harm the Party functionaries, their families, or their property. A lesson was learned: there was a vast difference between those who made the rules and those who had to follow them. The crowds had already started to disperse when looting and rioting broke out in the business sector of the city. This was not the usual pattern for worker protest as it had occurred in 1956 and 1970, where violence was aimed at official buildings and places of work not at stores or private businesses. This type of activity would be more inclined to alienate and anger the general populace then gain their support.

Security forces refused to intervene for some time but stood back taking hundreds of pictures of the crowds whether they were observing or taking part in the carnage. Fire hoses and tear gas were used to break up the riot only after several hours had elapsed. The security forces now had their excuse to crack down on the work force and their leadership in the riot torn cities. The fires and smoke had barely cleared away before the security police (*Urzad Bezpieczenstwa–U.B.*) began to round up workers in Radom and Ursus. People were arrested left and right whether they took part in the demonstrations or not. The security forces now had a chance to prove themselves and to show the Party that they were worth the extra pay that they were granted under the nomenklatura system. Individuals were dragged from their homes, their places of work, and off the streets. People were thrown into paddy wagons and driven to U.B. compounds where their ordeal was to begin. Several hundred people were arrested, an exact number is unknown, in both cities. When they arrived at the compounds, they were thrown out of the police vans to awaiting officers. Prisoners were ordered to run the "Path of Health": people were forced to run between rows of truncheon wielding police. Victims of this horrendous parody of jogging were beaten, kicked, and punched. From the "path," workers were dragged before a makeshift court to be tried for their offenses. The court was made up of security officers. The accused was brought before the court officers, told his crime, and then ordered to sign a statement that they were guilty of the crime. The accused was not permitted to defend himself or to voice any complaints over his treatment at the hands of the police. The punishments given out by these kangaroo courts ranged from stiff fines to extensive prison terms. Those who received only fines were permitted to leave and return to their homes or work. The torture did not end here though. Those prisoners that were freed were kept under constant surveillance by the security police.

The objective was to instill fear in them and others to prevent any further outbursts. Many workers who were arrested lost their places in worker hostels or were removed from apartment lists. Workers were fired from their jobs because of their arrest or their association with the protests. Management used articles 52 and 65 of the new 1974 labor code to justify the sacking of these laborers. The articles gave employers the right to fire anyone who was absent from work for unacceptable reasons or who disturbed the order and peace of a work place. Interpretation of who fell under these articles was left to the discretion of management. The breaking of these articles resulted in the nullification of a work contract. It is estimated that over one thousand people were fired in Radom and Ursus under these articles. The authorities continued to insist that "no Polish worker had been arrested or punished in any way for taking part in strikes or demonstrations."[1]

The people who fell under the attack of the authorities searched in vain for assistance from social services and the official unions to protect and defend them. Social service agencies refused to recognize the existence of this group of people since officially they did not exist. Official unions condemned the strikers as hooligans and antisocial elements who deserved no sympathy. Prepared speeches were issued to local union representatives throughout the country to condemn the workers of Radom and Ursus as well as others who instigated sit down strikes in other cities. Some union officials were fired from their positions for refusing to read the statement. Those who were suffering under the oppressive tactics of the authorities were not left to fend for themselves though. Some of the workers began to band together to aid their persecuted brethren with the assistance of a group of intellectuals and clergy that became known as the Workers' Defense Committee (*Komitet Obrony Robotnikow*—KOR). Lech Walesa stated in his Nobel Award speech in 1983 that the events of 1976 indicated an urgent need for solidarity amongst the workers and the rest of society for common protection. The next four years were to witness the growth of this solidarity throughout Polish society.[2]

The Workers' Defense Committee (KOR) was formed on September 23, 1976. KOR was only one of a number of human rights groups that formed from 1975 to 1980. The Movement for the Defense of Human and Civil Rights (ROPCiO) was formed in 1975 and was the other major civil rights group next to KOR. These groups were Polish variants of a wider movement for human rights throughout the entire Eastern Bloc, such as the Charter 77 group in Czechoslovakia and the various Helsinki Watch groups in the area. KOR and ROPCiO held several features that were uniquely Polish; the gulf between the radical intelligentsia, the workers, and the Catholic Church was bridged and there was a great emphasis placed on using the Polish constitution as a basis for their arguments and stance.

Jerzy Andrzejewski, author of Ashes and Diamonds, was one of twenty-four founding members of the Workers' Defense Committee. He argued that the reason for the formation of the Committee was that "society's only defense against lawlessness is solidarity and mutual support." Jacek Kuron, another founding member and political activist, said that KOR was formed not out of any lofty ideals but out of shame. The intelligentsia felt shame for their silence in 1970 and now hoped to regain some of their dignity by supporting the workers in their time of need. The protests that were carried out in June were done for the benefit of the whole nation, according to Jan Jozef Lipski, and those persecuted for their participation deserved the support of the nation.[3]

Jacek Kuron was well known to activists in Poland. He and Karol Modzelewski had sent an open letter to the Party twelve years earlier to protest the growing totalitarianism of the Party. In that letter, Kuron and Modzelewski argued for worker autonomy and democracy amongst a variety of other demands. Worker autonomy was to be actual rather than just an illusion. Autonomy had to go beyond the local factory level and the way to do this was through independent trade unions and workers' councils. It was up to the working class to set the goals of social production not the authorities. The workers' councils were to be the vehicles through which this was to be accomplished making them instruments of economic and eventual political power. The councils had to be truly elective with the ability of recall to be effective. Democracy had to be preserved to make them different from the institutions that already existed. In this sense, a plurality of working class parties had to exist free of interference and censorship to allow for the free exchange of ideas. Freedom of expression would be essential for a true workers' democracy argued Kuron. The organization of the working class in this manner was not to be revolutionary but evolutionary.[4]

Adam Michnik, another KOR founder and historian, also argued for evolution rather than revolution. Michnik chastised the intelligentsia for addressing their demands for change to the wrong people. A program for evolutionary change should be addressed to an independent public not to a totalitarian power that would resist any change. Pressure for change must come from below and the demands should be presented by the working class because it is they who the power elite fear most. This is a very important change in the perspective of the intelligentsia. Kuron's letter for change was addressed to the Party while Michnik's letter was addressed to society. Kuron and Michnik agreed that society had to come to the realization that they could make a difference and that ultimate power rested with them and not with the power elite. Society had to be taught to resist, to remain independent and distinct. Each act of resistance saves a portion of liberty and preserves the values without which a nation cannot survive. The key was to overcome the oppressor's greatest weapon and that was fear. Once man rose above that fear then one became a free person, an independent human being. The Party was not to be ignored in this attempt at change. Change from the Party was inevitable and should be welcomed but it would never be enough.

The Party pragmatist could be a partner with the democratic opposition but never an ally. The opposition had to remain separate and distinct if they did not want to be incorporated into the present system. All activities were to be open and above board. The ideas of Kuron and Michnik were not new but were a revival of much of the thought of the old Polish Socialist Party. The writings of these two men combined with basic Christian ethics such as truthfulness and renunciation of violence were to provide the platform for the Workers' Defense Committee. KOR was to attract a wide array of people into its ranks and was to lay a foundation for cooperation between the various social groups in Polish society.[5]

The organization of the Committee was never formal or rigid. It was an informal association of like minded people. The initial objectives of the group were to provide material, medical, and legal assistance to workers who had been arrested or were fired from their jobs and to distribute accurate information on the plight of the workers to the foreign news media. KOR held a defensive posture the first few weeks of its existence. They collected money and food for the families of imprisoned workers and provided workers with legal advice. ROPCiO also collected and distributed a large amount of money to worker families. KOR decided to go on the offensive by the end of September. The Committee began to organize laborers in Ursus and Radom to write collective letters to protest their treatment by police and demand reinstatement of their sacked coworkers. The letters were to be sent to the highest authorities in Poland including Edward Gierek. The main obstacle that the Committee had to overcome was fear of retribution for taking an independent stance. The letters were passed by hand in the factories secretly and were given only to workers who could be trusted not to divulge or destroy the letter. The letters were composed by worker activists with the assistance of KOR members. In total, over 3,000 signatures were collected to send to Gierek and others. The petitions went unanswered which was not unexpected. The objective of the letters was not necessarily to force the authorities into bending to the workers' demands but to make people take an independent stance and to break down the barrier of fear. The workers stood together against attempts to force people to retract their signatures. No dismissals from work, for signing the letter, occurred as a result of this collective stance.[6]

The Committee also began to print the *Biuletyn Informacjny* that fall,the objective of the *Biuletyn* was to break the "monopoly of information" by the authorities. KOR continually asked its supporters and readers for news of strikes, police brutality, and so on to show others that they were not alone in their suffering. They also reported on protest actions, other than strikes, to show people that they need not be helpless in the face of persecution. News reports had to be verified before they were published and if they were published it was done without editorial comment. This was done purposely so that KOR could not be accused of doctoring the facts and fall into the same category as the official press. This project was so successful that other independent journals began to spring up through out Poland. These journals were not only printed by human rights groups like KOR and ROPCiO but also by the workers themselves. The pressure put upon the authorities was to show some results early the next year.[7]

The government response to the growing opposition came on February 3, 1977. Edward Gierek asked for clemency for those workers still held in jail for their activities in June if they had shown repentance and given up their life of crime. He asked that their sentences be reduced or be suspended but never stricken from the records. This was to be a conditional suspension that could be retracted at the discretion of the authorities. The discretion clause left the former prisoners open to constant police harassment. It was to take six months before all those arrested were "freed." A questionable freedom was given to these people because coupled with this leniency was also a get tough policy by the police with the opposition. There was a renewed emphasis on the use of psychological terror on the workers and their supporters. Worker activists were constantly harassed by the security police at home, at work, and on the street. The whole process was meant to show the Polish people who was in charge in Poland—the Party.[8]

The authorities realized that the mere release of prisoners would not be sufficient to quiet the opposition or correct the problems surfacing in the economy and society. The government chose to see all of its problems as economic rather than having political connotations associated with them. The Gierek government introduced a variety of half-hearted changes in order to shore up its position. Authorities cut investments in heavy industry by 5 percent and attempted to shift this over to housing construction and consumer goods. An increase in investments in food production was also started to stimulate farming. For all the possible good intentions behind these rather weak reforms, they came to naught because no cverall plan for their implementation was introduced. The result of this haphazard approach was increased waste and confusion. The consumer market still lagged far behind consumer demand, especially in food stuffs, so that the government was forced to increase its food imports from the West which dwindled away much of its hard currency. Prices for food were still kept artificially low by the state so that out of every one hundred zlotys spent on food the state paid seventy zlotys. The heavy subsidization of food was not to last long because by 1978 prices began to increase quietly so that by 1979 they had gone up 30 percent. Despite the price increases shortages of products remained a constant source of frustration to all Poles. The queue on the streets in front of stores became a common sight and a common place to exchange complaints. A common joke at this time went:

> A man had been waiting in line for five hours. "I have had enough!" he suddenly exploded. "I am going to punch Gierek." Half an hour later he returned more frustrated than ever. 'What happened?' asked a friend. "No luck," he said "There they had a six hour line."

People could see the situation deteriorating around them. Coal also proved to be a short commodity over the winters so that entire cities were forced to go without heat and lights for long periods of time. Hospitals closed down due to a lack of supplies and drugs. At the same time, the authorities and the official media kept telling the people that things could not be better. *Tyrbuna Ludu* reported, on January 23, 1978, that all basic market quotas were overfilled for 1977 except for just a few areas such as food and clothing. As conditions and shortages grew worse in the country so did the propaganda of success. The evening television news became known as the "prosperity hour." Poles realized that the better things sounded the worse off they really were.[9]

Gierek tried to rebuild his support, especially amongst the working class but he proved incapable of the task. In his speeches and meetings with workers, he tended to vacillate between praise and scolding. He knew that he would have to regain some of their support if he was to remain in power. The Party, for now, was united behind Gierek out of fear of the population. For the most part this was probably justified. A poll of 2,800 workers in 1977, to find out the true feelings of the workers, revealed that the majority of the respondents believed that conflicts were inevitable and could not be solved through normal channels. Strikes were viewed as the best way to solve any problems by 40 percent of the respondents. Industrial sabotage was a favorite of ten per cent of the workers. More than half of the respondents felt that they were being exploited. Party activists knew that something had to be done to correct this growing ill will towards them. Gierek and his followers decided on two tactics to correct the problem; one was to try to make the workers feel more a part of the system and secondly to make the workers so subservient that they would not dare raise a hand against them.[10]

Gierek proclaimed at the seventh plenum of the Party's central committee that the "working class is the real master in our country." An affirmative action program aimed at recruiting blue collar workers into the Party was started to support Gierek's claim. The move proved relatively successful in that the number of workers in the Party increased but their ability to change anything remained the same. The workers remained in the lower echelons of the system while the power remained at the top. This proved to be more of a frustration than a cure.[11]

Gierek also promised a renewal of the unions and the self government bodies at the same time as the recruitment process was going on. These claims proved to be little more than cosmetic. While Gierek talked of making the workers comanagers of the economy, management's powers were increased to make them even more dominant over the two worker organizations. Many of the remaining powers of the trade unions and the workers' councils were transferred to management so that they became strictly vehicles of production stimulation and not labor representatives. In a speech before the second annual conference of the PUWP in 1978, Gierek stated that the objectives of the workers' councils were to raise the effectiveness and quality of output, organize work more effectively, raise the qualifications of the work force (education), and most of all improve labor discipline. The union's main function was to educate the labor force with a concern for efficiency and respect for management. These were the same duties described for both organizations in 1944. The key words were to work wisely, efficiently, and effectively. These words appeared in most of Gierek's speeches to the workers for the next two years.[12]

The self-management councils (KSRs) were ordered rejuvenated and reactivated as a sign of change. Workers' councils had by this time come to resemble Soviet style production councils. Membership in the KSRs was to be expanded so that at least one-third of the membership was to be made up of blue collar workers. The powers of the KSR were to remain the same. A well publicized letter was al o sent around to all enterprise directors reminding them of their obligations toward worker self-management. Gierek made the situation quite clear regarding the status of the KSRs when he spoke to their conferences in 1978 and 1979 and stated that their major concern was to aid management not interfere with it. Gone was the talk of comanagement. The workers did not take the bait of superficial change and the workers' councils began to fade from the economic scene. Membership dropped substantially between 1977 and 1978 so that by 1980 only six workers' councils remained in all of Poland, even the FSO factory near Warsaw which had a council since 1956 failed to elect one in 1980. KSRs were still viewed as manager's self government. The decline of interest in the KSRs did not go unnoticed in the official press. *Polityka* accused the KSR of being a facade and saw no point in maintaining it or the workers' councils since neither was trusted by the workers. *Zycie Warszawy* agreed that the councils should be dismantled since they were ignored anyway. Wieslaw Rogowski wrote in *Nowe Drogi* that worker self government would become effective only when working class interests converged with those of the rest of the community and the nation. Rogowski was describing what was happening in the free trade union movement.[13]

It was not until five months before the strike wave of 1980 that Gierek told a trade union plenum that their main task now was defense of the working people. This proclamation came shortly after the government had announced a period of coming austerity and harder work for the Polish people. The trade unions were to increase their impact on state policy and pay special attention to complaints of unjust distribution of wages and bonuses. This is the same ploy that was used between 1968 and 1970 by Wladyslaw Gomulka to buy off the workers. It did not work for Gomulka and it did not work for Gierek. By 1980, the workers had developed their own cadre of leadership through the founding committees of independent trade unions that were formed from 1978 to 1980. Gierek's facade of worker representation was to be eclipsed by these groups.[14]

The first attempt at independent worker action came in the fall of 1977. The movement centered around the creation of a journal aimed at the working class. The title of the new journal was *Robotnik*. The name *Robotnik* had historical precedent since it was also the former masthead of the old Polish Socialist Party publication, originally edited by Jozef Pilsudski, the founder of the modern Polish state. The editors of this new journal were trying to claim for themselves the old socialist heritage and traditions. *Robotnik* was meant to be different from the *Biuletyn Informacjny* in that the latter was intended for general and foreign consumption while the former was meant to be read by workers and was aimed at large industrial enterprises. The objective of the project was to inform people that they were not alone in their protests, to end the isolation of the individual and to organize them on a larger and much more cohesive scale than had been previously accomplished. The correspondents, editors, and distributors were laborers like the readers themselves. The intelligentsia only gave technical advice. The activists wanted to broaden the readers perspectives beyond that of the factory to show them that their problems were part and parcel with those of the rest of society.[15]

The first issue of the journal was poorly mimeographed and only four pages long. *Robotnik* was to have a run of only four hundred issues that first time. Within a year, it had expanded to twelve readable pages with a run of 20,000 copies and was published biweekly rather than in irregular editions. The journal became a chronicle of the everyday lives of workers and wound up having the widest circulation of all the independent publications in Poland. It was estimated that over 200,000 people read each edition and took to heart the closing lines of each edition: READ IT—PASS IT ON—DO NOT LET IT BE DESTROYED. *Robotnik* was so successful that it fostered local splinter journals such as *Robotnik Wybrzeza* (Worker of the Coast) in Gdansk and *Robotnik Szczecinski* (Szczecin Worker).[16]

Robotnik's first major accomplishment was to report on the strike wave of 1978. Strikes had become endemic to the Polish economy since 1976 but few people knew of them since the official press ignored such things. The journal's correspondents collected and collated data on the various strikes throughout the country and found that they were motivated out of self-defense. The strikers were trying to protect themselves against unjust wage reduction. The objectives of the 1978 strikes, as in the past, were not to gain new concessions from the authorities but retain what they already had. The journal reported that the majority of the strikes were initially successful in regaining lost benefits but once the situations quieted down and the strike committees dissolved then concessions were withdrawn and worker leaders were fired. The lessons learned from 1978 were that for a strike to be successful greater coordination and cooperation between different worker and societal groups was needed and to have long-lasting results a permanent independent worker organization would be necessary.[17]

Robotnik followed the strike wave news with the printing of a Charter of Worker's Rights. The charter gave a list of basic demands that covered wages, work hours, safety, the right to strike, and called for an end to special privileges for members of the *nomenklatura*. The document also presented five basic steps on how to achieve these rights: use the strike for short term goals; disseminate information; use the official trade unions when possible; keep workers alert and ready for action; and finally, and most importantly, form free trade unions. The charter was signed by one hundred worker activists from twenty–two cities from Gdansk to Zabrze. The list of signers read like a who's who of the future leadership of the independent trade union Solidarity. This document was to be a rallying point for the various founding committees of the free trade union movement in Poland.[18]

The training and organization of a leadership cadre for the labor movement began in the fall of 1977 in the city of Radom. A small group of individuals, a mixture of workers and intellectuals, formed the first trade union committee around the underground journal *Robotnik*. The creation of this committee was quickly followed up by the formation of another committee in Katowice, a large mining center. The free trade union movement in Silesia was started strictly by workers. Wladyslaw Sulecki, a well known activist miner, and Kazimierz Switon, a radio mechanic, provided the leadership for the group. Other founding members were electricians, miners, welders, and mechanics. The initial membership was small but they felt that they were strong enough to make an impact in the region. The miners of Silesia were quite unhappy with the servility of the official trade unions and workers' councils. Even the official trade union journal, *Gornik*, attacked the union leadership as being too subservient to management. The objectives of the founding committee were to operate openly, not as part of an underground, to provide role models to show the less active workers that it was possible to defend themselves, and to stand up for the rights of the workers. The first campaign of the Silesian free trade union movement was to organize the miners to demand free Sundays and a forty-hour work week. Switon and the others received enough support to force the authorities into giving the miners free Sundays. The authorities did not officially recognize the free trade unions but gave them tacit recognition by giving into part of their demands. The unions activities did not stop there.

Members continued to write letters on behalf of other workers, publish informational pamphlets, and generally show support for workers interests. Open activities brought retaliation from the authorities. Arrests, beatings, and general harassment became part of the everyday lives of Switon, Sulecki, and others. Switon was even attacked and beaten upon leaving mass one Sunday morning. The threat of physical punishment did not deter the union leadership but only made them more determined to continue. They even went so far as to send a telegram to Soviet Party Chairman Leonid Brezhnev to protest the arrest and mistreatment of a Russian free trade unionist.[19]

The Workers' Defense Committee took great interest in the Katowice union movement. They offered their advice and support to the fledgling union. The unionists appreciated the support but not always the advice. Jacek Kuron was very critical of the activities of Switon and the others. Kuron felt that they had begun their activities prematurely before receiving the support of the local workers. Switon was angered by what he viewed as KOR's attempt to ridicule and dominate their union movement. There was still a lot of latent animosity and distrust between the workers and the intellectuals dating back to 1970 and 1956. Many workers still viewed the intelligentsia as a pampered class, the privilegentsia, who only wished to use the laboring class for their own ends. The workers' distrust was to abate to some degree in 1980 when they took over the leadership of the opposition movement.[20]

The Katowice free union movement influenced the formation of other such organizations. The founding committee of the Baltic Free Trade Union movement was created in May of 1978. The founding members were again workers; an engineer and two construction workers. They were to echo the same concerns that the Katowice group had four months earlier. The stated objectives of the Gdansk group were the protection of workers regardless of political views and the regaining of the right of self-determination. The Gdansk committee proved to be very active and more open to cooperation with the intelligentsia than their predecessors. They like the group in Katowice chose open activities and started their work with a protest over a new wage system that was to be introduced. This proved to be only the beginning. They went on to organize, with the assistance of the local intelligentsia, educational classes on labor history, law, and a wide variety of other topics. The system that was developed was very similar to the prewar labor colleges that had existed in Poland. The most extensive project that they undertook was to print a local version of *Robotnik* called *Robotnik Wybrzeza* (Worker of the Coast). Copies of the paper found their way into factories, trams, trains, and churches. The workers in the area would often hear of wage changes or other pertinent information in *Robotnik Wybrzeza* before they would hear about it at work. The paper had a direct result in the calling of a strike in the shipyards of Gdansk in the fall of 1979 when it published news of a drastic wage reduction by the end of the year.[21]

The open activities of the Gdansk group brought the same response from the authorities in that city that it did in Katowice. Lech Walesa, one of the earliest members, found it very hard to keep a job or stay out of jail as a result of his activities. Those who defended members of the free trade union movement found themselves demoted or sacked. Anna Walentynowicz, another early member of the Gdansk group, was ostracized at work. Workers were forbidden to speak to her and her department head followed her throughout the day to ensure that she spoke to no one. Walentynowicz and Walesa were not the only ones to suffer harassment as a result of their work. One activist, Jan Szczepanski, was murdered by "unknown" assailants after being released from police custody for attending a free union meeting. The atrocities of the security police did not deter the work of the union activists who became more determined to succeed with each new adversity.[22]

The Gdansk group became the most active and most visible of the free trade union organizations in Poland. Members began to take over the role of leadership of the opposition movement in the region from KOR and the other human rights groups. In 1978, KOR and ROPCiO organized a memorial service on December 17 to honor those who fell in the 1970 protests. The following year, the service was run by the free trade union movement of Gdansk. The service was held at Gate no. 2 and approximately 6,000 people came to honor the dead. A brief wreath laying ceremony was conducted and then four speeches were delivered, one by Lech Walesa a former member of the 1970 strike committee. He told the crowd that they must learn from history and the mistakes made there. "We must learn to defend ourselves and our leaders." The way to do this was to organize permanent structures to demand our rights and protect our people. The meeting was concluded with the singing of "God Save Poland" the hymn sung during the Russian occupation of Poland in the nineteenth century. Several organizers were arrested after the memorial service but were freed when a strike was threatened at the shipyards. News of the success of the gathering spread quickly through the underground press and as a result other memorial gatherings were held in Warsaw, Poznan, Legnica, Wroclaw, Kalisz, and for the first time in Szczecin. The quick spread and wide popularity of these services was evidence of the growing discontent amongst the people and the rise of a group people willing to take the lead in breaking the cycle of fear.[23]

The strikes of late 1979 early 1980 began to take on a noneconomic character as a result of the influence of the free trade union movement. The protests were no longer aimed only at the changing of work norms or food shortages but now also against the repression of workers and solidarity with those who were being persecuted (workers or not). This kind of strike was most evident in Gdansk and in the shipbuilding industries. A good example of this kind of protest occurred when Anna Walentynnowicz was to be fired for her participation in the December memorial services. Several work stoppages took place throughout the Lenin Shipyards when news of her dismissal reached the shop floor. Eighty percent of her department refused to go back to work until she was rehired. Walentynowicz was reinstated as a result of the strikes. Other workers were similarly protected from arbitrary dismissal because of their political activities. Another aspect of this growth of independent activity was the rise of workers' commissions.[24]

Illegal workers' commissions began to form spontaneously in early 1980. Members were not elected but self nominated. They initially operated secretly and only slowly moved into open activities. One such commission was formed at Elektromontaz under the leadership of Lech Walesa. It began to operate in the open when twenty-five workers were fired from their jobs for political reasons. The commission came to their defense, taking over the role of the shop union. The commission demanded the reinstatement of the sacked workers and called for a solidarity rally to show labor's support of their colleagues. The factory management backed down and rehired the twenty-five workers. The five man commission then demanded that all future dismissals be countersigned by them. A dual power structure system was starting to form and receive the support of the majority of workers in a number of enterprises. The independent activities of the workers was spreading and intensifying.[25]

The growth of the independent opposition movement throughout all of Polish society in the late 1970s can be only partially attributed to the decline in the Polish economy. The election of Karol Wotyla as Pope in 1978 was of even greater influence than the growing lines at the markets upon the minds of the Polish people. These people who had struggled for so long and had steadfastly stood by the Roman Catholic church now felt as if their faith had been rewarded. The Church did not demand this loyalty but earned it by remaining true to the Polish nation. The Church had become the main supporter of human rights in Poland and it became especially active after the events of 1976. The lower clergy were members and supporters of the Workers' Defense Committee. Cardinal Stefan Wyszynski, himself, took up the defense of the workers in his Sunday sermons. He told the crowds that came to listen to his words that it was painful to see workers have to struggle for their rights in a workers' state. He joined KOR in calling for the freeing of prisoners and the creation of a true and honest dialogue between the people and the authorities.

> How can a nation live when basic human rights were denied it? A nation that has no human rights is not a nation, but a collection of soulless robots.

Spiritual and material support for the workers from the Church coincided with the help given by KOR and the other human rights groups. Churches were often used as meeting places for these groups. Cooperation and dialogue between the intelligentsia and the Church had begun as early as 1968 when the Church was the sole voice of support for the intellectual protests that year. Adam Michnik became a most avid supporter of cooperation with the Church although he was not a believer himself. He referred to the Church as the key source of encouragement to all people. He was one of the first to recognize that the Church had taken an anti-totalitarian stance since 1944 and that the opposition had a lot to learn from this experience. The intelligentsia's new found respect for the church was a complete about face from their old stance of viewing the clergy as the harborers of conservatism and reactionism.[26]

The election of a Polish Pope in 1978 did much to raise the prestige of the Polish Church and create a spiritual renewal amongst the entire nation. The burst of national pride that Poland was to feel in 1978 turned into an explosion when the Pope came home in 1979. It is estimated that over 10,000,000 people came to hear him speak. He was to make three dozen public appearances and was to show the world who the true leader of Poland was. A quarter of a million people attended a mass for the working people of Poland at Czestochowa, Poland's holiest shrine. Workers came from all over the country to show their respect and affection. The massive crowd was told that "It is the mission of the Church to make man more confident, more courageous, and conscious of his rights." He told the crowds not to be afraid of threats but to fear cowardice and indifference. "Christ protested against the degradation of man even through his work. Man is not a mere production tool that can be grouped, valued, and assessed." Man's place was above this. Adam Michnik wrote that the greatest accomplishment of the Pope's visit was that it gave Poles a sense of dignity and identity, a feeling that they were not alone in their beliefs. Kazimierz Brandys agreed when he wrote in his *Warsaw Diary*, "He came to lift us out of the mud." The people began to believe in themselves and that they were capable of doing anything. A renewed feeling of self reliance rather than desperation spread throughout the country. The government need no longer be approached for changes in society, the Polish people could do it themselves. While all this was going on, Edward Babiuch, the Polish Prime Minister, was writing in the *World Marxist Review* that the Polish United Workers Party had won the confidence and support of the working people.[27]

While Edward Babiuch was telling the Marxist world that labor was solidly behind the Party, sociologists and others were telling a different story. A totally different perspective of life was given by sociologists based on two sets of interviews conducted with workers throughout the country in 1979. The majority of the blue collar workers saw Polish society in dichotomous terms: we versus the authorities. Blue collar workers proved to be the most radical of all those questioned. They demanded such changes as economic egalitarianism, worker's autonomy, and effective management. They described their anger as the result of a feeling of downward mobility and frustration over the inability to meet their basic needs. Instead of relief, Poles were told that inflation was rising by 8 percent while national income was falling by 2 percent. The Experience and Future Group, a collection of Party and non-Party intellectuals, warned that if viable changes were not introduced soon an explosion was imminent. It was no longer a question of whether a social outburst would come but when would it come. Party sociologists, at a meeting at Jablonna in 1979, agreed that the best way to deal with such an explosion would be for the Polish military and police to crush it without Soviet assistance. The scenario was now set for the summer of 1980 and beyond.[28]

Chapter Four

We Are Not Comrades, We Are Citizens!

Food prices were to rise again in July of 1980. The workers initial response was to call a local strike, get quick concessions and then get back to work, but by mid-August their approach had changed. No longer were the strikes local in nature but were now regional and eventually national in character. Strike committees from city to city began to coordinate their activities with the main strike committee formed in Gdansk. The demands of the strikers expanded beyond economic concerns to social and even political reform. The workers were at the forefront of a social revolution much to the surprise of the other social groups in Poland including the Party. The Church, the intelligentsia, and the peasantry began to coalesce around the workers and looked to them for leadership. The workers in turn became the defenders of Polish culture and the Polish nation.

On July 1, 1980, food prices were again raised by the government. Meat prices rose from 90 to 100 percent. The price increases were actually started weeks earlier but very quietly. The increased revenue was to aid pensioners and low-wage employees according to the official press release. The response of the workers, in the larger cities, was a strike wave which spread throughout the entire country. Initially, the strikes remained localized with only limited objectives such as pay raises or food bonuses. They were spontaneous and generally unorganized. The Worker's Defense Committee (KOR) declared that it would act as a strike information center for the country. This information was spread through the paper *Robotnik* to workers throughout the country.[1]

The largest of the July strikes was to occur in the industrial city of Lublin, in southeastern Poland. On July 11, the strike wave that had already hit Ursus and towns near Gdansk now swamped Lublin. Twenty factories were to go on strike that first week. By the second week, a general strike was called for the entire city and an interfactory strike was organized to negotiate with the local authorities. Attention was quickly drawn to the area when railway engineers abandoned their trains taking food and other commodities to the Soviet Union. Authorities soon began to pay attention to the protest. The strike committee put forth only basic economic demands (pay raises, increased food supplies, etc.) which the government negotiators were quick to accept. The authorities were surprised with the speed, organization, and unity showed by the workers in Lublin. The strikes did not end here, though. The number of strikes was to increase to 150 across Poland by the end of July. Just as one strike ended, another would start somewhere else in the country. The strike became an unofficial way to bargain. In the face of rising opposition, the Party tried to call a halt to the growing chaos.[2]

The official press had little to say about the strikes and their effects. One had to read between the lines to realize that something was going on. *Trybuna Ludu* and other papers were filled with pleas for increased productivity, fulfillment of labor's patriotic duties, and concern for the increased interest among Poland's "friends" as to the state of the Polish economy. Gierek told reporters that "we shall continue our present line in the current and coming year." Discipline and hard work would save the day. Denial of the problem did not make it go away. The Party was forced to admit by August 12 that strikes had taken place. Jerzy Lukaszewicz told the foreign press that negotiations were now being carried out with various worker groups throughout the country to settle the misunderstandings that had arisen. What the propaganda minister did not know at the time was that within two days a strike would hit Gdansk which would have national and international repercussions and that within twelve days he would lose his job.[3]

At 6 a.m. on August 14, the electricians of departments K1 and K3 of the Lenin shipyards, in Gdansk, put down their tools and agreed to go on strike. Soon the engine construction section (C5) joined the strike. The groundwork for this strike had been laid weeks earlier by the Coastal Free Trade Union Movement by distributing leaflets and organizing private discussions in regards to calling a strike. By 9 a.m. a strike committee was formed. Only modest demands were made: the reinstatement of Anna Walentynowicz, who had just been fired because of her connection to the free trade union movement, and a wage increase of 1,000 zlotys. The plant manager, Klemens

Gniech, met with the strikers and offered to discuss their requests only if work was resumed. The crowd seemed ready to accept these promises and return to work when a short mustachioed man jumped onto the platform with the manager. Lech Walesa was that man.

Walesa, a former employee of the Lenin shipyards, had been smuggled into the yard when the strike was breaking up. When he saw that the workers were willing to give up the work stoppage for only promises of talks, he took the initiative. The workers in the yard knew him because of his work in the trade unions, the reason for his termination four years earlier. Walesa verbally attacked the manager and admonished the crowd for accepting such meager concessions from management. He then called for a general strike at the shipyards which met with overwhelming support. Walesa gave the strike a single identifiable leader who was trusted by the majority of the workers.[4]

Negotiations began immediately between management and the newly formed strike committee. The authorities were represented by Gniech and Tadeusz Fiszbach, the Gdansk Party Secretary. The tone of the meetings was set when Fiszbach addressed the crowds as "Comrades!" and he was shouted down by the workers yelling "We are not comrades! We are citizens!" The workers' initial demands were for the erection of a memorial to the victims of the 1970 Baltics strikes, reinstatement of Walentnowicz and Walesa, pay raises, better social insurance benefits and pensions, publication of their demands in the local newspaper, and the creation of free trade unions in the shipyards. Negotiations were carried out for two days in the main conference center. The public address system broadcast the proceedings over the entire shipyard. Gniech offered a complicated system of pay scales which would have given some workers a greater pay increase then others, a poor attempt to split the workers. This offer was turned down. The strike committee wanted all employees to get an equal share.[5]

While these negotiations were going on, other factories in the Gdansk region also went on strike; the Paris Commune shipyard in Gdynia (led by Andrzej Kolodziej, a former worker at the Lenin yards), the Northern Repair shipyards, the dock workers, public transport, and other smaller industries connected to the shipping industry.

On August 16, a tentative settlement was reached at the Lenin yards. The management agreed to pay increases, a memorial to the strikes of 1970, and the reinstatement of sacked workers. The workers felt that this was the best that they could get from the authorities. Walesa had already announced the end of the strike when workers from around Gdansk converged on the Yard to request that they maintain a sympathy strike until their agreements had been signed. The majority of the Lenin workers wanted to keep the solidarity strike. The strike committee scrapped the tentative agreement and agreed to continue the strike. "We must not betray the other strikers. We must fight alongside them till the end" Walesa told the crowd.[6]

On the night of August 16, the Interfactory Strike Committee (MKS) was formed. Twenty–one factories and enterprises initially made up the MKS. The working committee was made up of two representatives from each of the striking units. The goal of the MKS was to coordinate the demands and the strike actions of the associated factories and enterprises. The MKS was not to dissolve at the end of strike but was to remain as a monitoring device to insure the implementation of the demands and to organize free trade unions. A new list of demands was drawn up which now included an end to censorship, the freeing of political prisoners, a ceiling on maximum wages, standardization of wages for similar jobs and skills throughout the country, the abolition of piecework payments, increases in pensions and welfare funds, longer maternity leaves, the upgrading of health services, and the liquidations of special privileges for Party favorites. Gniech refused to recognize the MKS and cut the electricity to their meeting hall. Leaflets were dropped on the yard to persuade the workers to end the strike. Fiszbach accused the workers of being duped by antisocialist elements. By August 18, over 156 factories and plants were associated with the Gdansk MKS.[7]

The day after the strike in Gdansk started, Prime Minister Edward Babiuch went on television on the Baltic Coast to plead with the workers to go back to their jobs. He tried to convince them that they were only harming themselves with the strike. He tried to impress on his audience that Poland's allies were becoming very concerned over the situation and that they wished the Poles success in overcoming their difficulties "from the bottom of their hearts." Babiuch's speech proved to be very similar to the speech given to the Lublin workers a few weeks earlier and very similar to statements made in 1956 to 1976. The local newspaper *Glos Wybrzeza* followed Babiuch's speech with accusations that the strikes were being led by outsiders hostile to socialism. The greatest tirade leveled against the strikers came from Jan Szydiak, the head of the official unions Central Committee, when he called the protests acts of hostility against the state and declared that the organizers were nothing more than terrorists. He made it quite clear that "We will not give up power or share it."[8]

Gierek went on television to speak to the people and hopefully calm the situation as he had done in the past. He addressed his audience as "dear fellow citizens." He pleaded with them to remain calm and resume work. He asked for reason and moderation and an end to the strikes which were only multiplying Poland's difficulties. The Party chairman promised to give all demands serious thought and consideration. The streamlining and restructuring of the official unions was to be a top priority of the Party but only after the strikes had ceased. Gierek's speech lasted twenty-five minutes but few in the Lenin shipyards heard it. Most of them were attending mass.[9]

The Party was not unanimous in its assessment of the situation in Poland. Many Party members, mostly low-level ones supported, even led, the strikes in various factories. Tadeusz Fiszbach was one of the first high-level Party members to recognize publicly the Lenin Shipyard strike as an "authentic protest of the working class." Fiszbach organized a committee to compile a list of worker demands and then submit proposals to Warsaw on how to meet them. The proposals called for improvements in working conditions, social welfare benefits, and economic management. The proposals did not go as far as the workers', but Party reformers had now joined in the chorus of workers and the intelligentsia calling for reforms. Fiszbach presented the same proposals to the government negotiating committee when it arrived in Gdansk on August 19.[10]

Prime Minister Babiuch was asked formally by the MKS to open negotiations on August 19. In response to this request, Vice Premier Tadeusz Pyka was sent to Gdansk to open talks with the workers. Pyka took with him Henryk Jablonski, president of the Polish People's Republic, and Stanislaw Kania, head of state security. The vice-premier first met with the local Party leader and then went to talk to the workers. He refused to recognize the MKS and began meeting with individual enterprises. Seventeen factories opened talks with the Pyka commission but broke them off when they were asked to renounce the MKS. After this incident, no other enterprise would meet with the government commission. Pyka was replaced by Mieczyslaw Jagielski, also a vice-premier.[11]

On August 21, Jagielski met with a three-man delegation from the MKS which now represented 400 striking units. The MKS set down two preconditions before any negotiations could start; one was formal recognition of the MKS as the sole representative of the Gdansk strikers and second, an end to the communications blackout of the region which had started a week earlier. Jagielski agreed to these conditions only if Walesa, Walentynowicz, and Andrzej Gwiazda (another free trade unionist) were removed from the presidium of the Interfactory Strike Committee. The delegation refused the request and only after several hours of talks did Jagielski remove his demand and accept the MKS preconditions outright. It was agreed that negotiations would begin in two days at the Lenin shipyards.[12]

By mid-August, the entire city of Gdansk was run by the strikers. All essential public services were in the hands of the workers and continued to function normally throughout the strike. Everything from the bakeries to taxis operated smoothly under worker supervision. Even the Zomo (security police) had to request gasoline from the strikers when they ran short. All liquor sales were banned in the city to prevent outbreaks of violence. A worker's militia was also formed to patrol the streets and maintain security in the factories. The striker summed up the mood of all the others when he said "Nobody is misbehaving. This is no time for fun. We're all in this together . . . not a mob . . . just workers involved in a peaceful protest."[13]

Many of the intelligentsia did not foresee the power or the discipline of the workers. At first, they thought that any actions by labor would be chaotic and even destructive. When the strikes proved calm with clear objectives, the intelligentsia were forced to change their minds. As the strike in Gdansk progressed, they decided to associate themselves with it. The question presented to the intellectuals was what position would they take in the protest. Would they become directors of the protest or submit to the leadership of the strike committees? While the debate went on, a group of intellectuals from Warsaw appeared at the Lenin Shipyards offering their services as advisors to the MKS.[14]

The intelligentsia arrived from Warsaw two days before the negotiations were to begin. The group was led by Tadeusz Mazowiecki of the Catholic Intellectual Club and included sociologists, economists, and historians. Walesa and the MKS gladly accepted their offer of assistance. Walesa told Mazowiecki and Bronislaw Geremek, a historian, that "We know what we want but you are better at putting it into words." A commission of experts was set up to advise the presidium. Each member of the presidium became a specialist in his own right; Gwiazda on trade unions, Walentynowicz on political prisoners, Alina Pienkowska for health, and Lech Badkowski on censorship. Walesa became the coordinator of the committee. Out of these specialists grew the final draft of the twenty-one demands. The formal title of the twenty-one points was "The Task of the Enterprises and Institutions on Strike represented by the Interfactory Strike Committee in Session at the Gdansk Shipyard." The final petition included demands for the right to strike, freedom of speech, the freeing of political prisoners, more religious freedom, wage increases, a call for an end to special privileges on the basis of *nomenklatura*, improvements in working conditions and pensions, increased child care and maternity benefits, and free trade unions. These were the demands presented to vice-premier Jagielski on August 26.[15]

On the day before Jagielski arrived, pictures of John Paul II and red and white Polish flags began to sprout from the gates of the Lenin Shipyards. Inside, one could see men and women going to confession or listening to a mass said by Bishop Kaczmarek of the Gdansk diocese. Symbols out of Poland's forbidden past also began to appear. Strikers began to wear red and white armbands reminiscent of the Warsaw Uprising of 1944 and pictures of Josef Pilsudski, recognized as the founder of the modern Polish state and an anticommunist, began to be seen in prominent places. The workers began to take on the mantle of leaders and preservers of Polish society. "We are not fighting for a mere pittance for ourselves but for justice for the whole nation" said one worker. They were putting into practice the slogan that so many Poles before them had "For your freedom and ours."[16]

Jagielski and his team of experts arrived at the shipyards to be greeted by Walesa and the presidium on the morning of August 26. The authorities anticipated talking their way around any concrete agreements but found the workers quite capable negotiators. The presidium told Jagielski that "Poles were sick to death of listening to talk of errors and mistakes which go on being repeated." Talks went on for four days. Every point was agreed upon except the demand for free trade unions. Jagielski refused to even discuss the subject.[17]

When the negotiations seemed to hit a snag over the free trade union question, the authorities tried a variety of tactics which had worked in the past to break the solidarity of the workers. Four members of the Politburo were sacked including Edward Eabiuch, the prime minister, and Jan Szydlak, the trade union chairman. The offering of scapegoats proved to have little effect. A common response from the workers was that the Polish people were tired of the Party's musical chairs. New, democratic, trade union elections were promised and Walesa was approached to head the new trade union's central committee. Walesa politely refused the bribe offered to him and the workers ignored the offers of new personnel without structural changes in the official unions. The possibility of military action was even discussed but discounted due to the questionable loyalty of the army conscripts. The final factor that forced the authorities to give into the demand for free trade unions came when the miners of the powerful Silesian coal region went on strike in support of the Gdansk demands.[18]

As a compromise, the Gdansk workers agreed to abide by the constitution of the Polish People's Republic, which recognized the leading role of the Polish United Worker's Party in the state. With this assurance, Jagielski agreed to the final demand for free trade unions. The final proposal was signed on Saturday, August 30. Work resumed in most factories of the MKS the following Monday.[19]

The Polish government may have had good intentions when they signed that historic agreement on August 31, but applying the various aspects of the compromise was not to prove easy. The Polish economy was in sorry shape and was not capable of bearing much strain at this time. Disagreements were to rise between the new union and the government as to how fast the Gdansk agreement should be applied. The government envisioned a long range application while the union looked for a more immediate response to their demands. The government made its first gesture towards the workers within two weeks of the strikes end.

On September 14, the Polish government formally announced that independent trade unions could exist and issued a list of procedures that had to be followed to be legally registered. Three days later, the MKS met in Gdansk to draw up the official statutes for the Independent Self-managed Trade Unions (NSZZ). Five hundred representatives from seventeen regional union federations gathered to form a national commission and adopt a formal structure for the new federation.

The choosing of a commission proved to be a simple task in that they kept the original MKS commission that was formed in the August strike. What proved to be a problem was deciding on a structure for the new federation. Delegates from the small factories and towns pushed for a strong centrally-controlled union, while the delegates from the coast and the more developed regions pushed for a loose federation. The centralist position argued for a strong union out of fear of being abandoned by the more powerful enterprises. They wanted a single strong union to support them and their objectives, an all protective umbrella. The decentralist or federation position pushed for loose contacts between various unions whose actions would be coordinated by an advisory commission. The federalists wanted all union members to live through the experience of forming and running their own local unions. This experience would be necessary if all union members were to appreciate what the strikes of August had won. The object was to learn self-reliance not switch rulers. Many of the smaller towns and enterprises had never gone on strike and were now trying to use the new union to substitute for the struggle and experience necessary to tie a group of people together. The objective of the new union was to rekindle autonomous public activity, not replace it. Participatory democracy was the goal.[20]

A compromise between the two positions was reached although the federalist position was given greater adherence. A direct opposite approach from democratic centralism was taken. Initiative was to come from below rather than from above. The national leadership was to provide only a coordinating role for the initiatives from the ranks. The various union districts were to have great autonomous powers. The union thus became a federation but with the potential to act as one unified body if the situation arose.

The new labor federation was to be composed of seventeen autonomous districts and under them, thirty–nine regions. The basic unit was to be the factory commission while the top was the National Coordinating Commission (KKP). The new union structure resembled the *sejmiki* (little parliaments) of the classic Polish nobility (*Szlachta*) and the workers also inherited their fanatical devotion to democratic procedure from the *Szlachta*.[21]

The only thing left to decide on was a name for the new federation. After much debate, it was decided that the name *Solidarnosc* (Solidarity) be given to the new union. Father Josef Tischner stated most eloquently the reasons for the choice of such a name as Solidarity.

> The word Solidarity binds people together, people who only yesterday were far apart. We are bound to each other even if we do not know it. It is born out of goodwill and awakens

goodwill in human beings . . . a communion of working people.

The final draft of the statutes was agreed upon on September 12 and, two days later, Walesa left for Warsaw to deposit the statutes for legal approval. While Solidarity waited for legal recognition, the union began to organize itself by setting up offices, putting out bulletins, and enrolling new members.[22]

Five days after the Gdansk agreement was signed, Edward Gierek fell ill and was rushed to a hospital. Gierek had suffered a heart attack just as his predecessor, Gomulka, had done ten years earlier. A new Party secretary was named to replace the ailing Gierek. Stanislaw Kania, the former chief of internal security, was named the new Party chief. Kania promised a return to Leninist norms and the correction of the grave mistakes made in the implementation of fundamentally correct policies. The problem lay in the leadership, not the system. He promised a new humble and consultative style of leadership. The Polish people saw nothing new in these changes or in the promises of their new leader. They had seen it all before in 1956, 1970, and 1976. A disgruntled worker put it very distinctly when he said "their musical chairs don't mean anything to us."[23]

The Party began to fear the growth of a dual power situation in Poland similar to what had existed in 1917 between the Soviets and the Provisional government. They had seen the scenario before, only now they were playing the part of Kerensky. The authorities often times tried to hinder the formation of independent unions through harassment, threats, and sometimes violence. Warnings were being sounded in the official press to gain sway over this new power base or lose control of the situation for good. Mieczslaw Rakowski, editor of *Polityka*, warned Solidarity that it was their duty to adapt to the system and not the system to it. He also advocated outright interference in the internal affairs of Solidarity to make sure the situation remained in hand. *Trybuna Ludu* suggested the same thing when they encouraged Party members to join Solidarity and become active in their affairs. The Party even tried reviving the official trade union structure under a new name.[24]

The official unions took their cues from the Party's leaders. They followed the set formula of changing their leadership and then making vague promises of change without structural or functional alterations. The old unions began to change their names to independent and self-managed just as Solidarity claimed to be. Members were promised more democracy and greater autonomy if only they would remain loyal to the state-sponsored unions. To show they meant business, the central committee of the trade union council was dismissed including Jan Szydlak, the most militant critic of the August protests. Szydlak was accused of errors and arbitrariness. The fault was not in the system but those running it, again. The new central committee sent out flyers to its 40,000 affiliates calling for some reform. The new chairman of the Council, Romuald Jankowski, pleaded with the workers not to abandon them.

> If you don't approve of the old union officials elect new ones. If you don't think we look after your interests properly, then help us change our policy. We are still worthy of your support and confidence. We will not accept the title of government unions.

Jankowski's first speech was given standing next to a bust of Lenin while Walesa's first speech was next to portraits of the Pope and Josef Pilsudski. The whole process was a desperate ploy by the old unions to hang on by using promises and semantics to confuse the Polish workers. The changes were not viewed seriously and the official unions were described as "old wine in new bottles." Zbigniew Bujak, head of the Solidarity Mazowsze region, stated that cooperation between the old and new unions was quite possible and would only benefit the working class, but the old unions would have to prove themselves to be something other than tools of management before they would be taken seriously.[25]

The new union did not always meet with opposition from Party members. Solidarity was often supported by local Party cells made up of rank and file members. The lower echelons of the Party were just as disgruntled with the system as Solidarity was. The rank and file disliked being ignored by the upper Party apparatus. An anti-apparatus movement was formed in the city of Torun soon after the strikes ended in September. The movement was organized by Zbigniew Iwanow, a long-time union member and an organizer of the August strike in Torun, also a Party Member. Iwanow was elected first secretary of his enterprise Party cell. The objective of the movement was to change the functions and operations of the PUWP. Election rules were to be changed to cut the power of the apparatus in the Party and particularly in the central committee in Warsaw. They wanted to prevent nonelected officials from making political decisions. They wanted to separate Party functions from state functions. They also demanded the right to form separate political platforms within the Party. In short, they wanted to introduce pluralism and democracy into the Party and break the power of the ruling clique. A consultative commission was created to facilitate inter-enterprise contacts, horizontalism rather than democratic centralism. This horizontalism was a direct attack on the leadership of the Party. Support for the movement spread to thirty–two enterprises in seventeen districts. Just as the group was gaining momentum, Warsaw began to crack down on it. Those associated with it were accused of losing their *Partyjnosc* (Party spirit). Members began to lose their jobs and were expelled from the Party. Iwanow, himself, was asked to turn in his Party card for allegedly receiving communion during the August strike. Kania denounced the group as confrontationalists trying to split the Party. The remaining members of the anti-apparatus movement were finally silenced at the Party congress in 1981.[26]

By the end of September, Solidarity had received no response on its application for legalization from the Warsaw court. A one-hour warning strike was decided upon for October 3 to prod the government into action. The call for the strike came first from the Coordinating Commission (KKP) in Gdansk and then was supported by the local unions, each one voting on whether to take part in the strike or not. The strike was to be "a manifestation of our strength, our sense of responsibility, and our discipline." Walesa told the membership:

> We must show that during this strike we will be capable of maintaining calm, order, the protection of public property, as well as affecting a return to normal working conditions.

The strike was a success throughout the entire country. It proved most successful in Gdansk where the entire city came to a halt from 12 to 1 o'clock on the day of the protest. In those places where it was not possible to stop, the workers would wear red and white armbands to show their solidarity. Walesa was quite pleased with the results in that they showed the authorities not only their unity, but also their ability to put it to use. The government was put on notice that if a decision on the registration of Solidarity was not soon in coming, the next step would be a general strike.[27]

Three weeks after the warning, the Warsaw district court handed down its decision to register Solidarity but with an added clause that stated the union recognized the PUWP and its leading role in the new unions. Solidarity refused to accept this decision and immediately filed an appeal with the Warsaw Supreme Court. On October 30, Walesa and his advisors arrived in Warsaw to start talks over this new obstacle with Jozef Pinkowski, the new prime minister. The union demanded the removal of the new clause and the formal acceptance of the Solidarity statutes as originally submitted. The union also called for greater access to the communications media, faster pay raises, better distribution of food, the end of union harassment by the ZOMO, and the recognition of the peasants' right to form a trade union. With this last item, Solidarity expanded its umbrella of protection to include the peasantry along with the intelligentsia and the Church. The talks ended with no formal settlement except that both sides would abide by the Supreme Court's decision which was to be delivered in two weeks.[28]

The KKP in the meantime called for a general strike on November 12 if Solidarity was not registered by then. Preparations were made to hold a rotating general strike which was to involve two cities a day for a week, starting with Gdansk and Warsaw. At the end of one week, the entire country would go on strike until the union was registered. Walesa described this as a controlled general strike. Regional strike committees instructed their members to bring food and bedding with them to work on the day of the strike and to be prepared for a prolonged occupation strike. Various threats and accusations were leveled at Solidarity by the government as the deadline grew closer and the workers showed that they were not going to back down. With two days to spare, the Supreme court handed down its decision.[29]

The Supreme Court overturned the district court's decision and agreed to register Solidarity under its original charter. The union, as a sign of compromise, did attach an addenda to the charter which stated Solidarity would abide by the Polish Constitution which recognized the leading role of the Party in the State. The union was now formally registered and could carry on the business of organizing itself legally. Walesa declared to a crowd of well-wishers, outside the court, "We have won what we set out for."[30]

The first great crisis, over registration, did great damage to the fledgling union. It gave rise to a group of union militants through the process of brinkmanship that was practiced on both sides. It gave some militants the idea that the authorities were no more than paper tigers that could be blown over at the union's will. These people began to raise the questions of whether it was wise to deal with such a government or even trust such a government. As Solidarity's power became more evident, factions within the union began to become more pronounced. The split between moderates and militant radicals, which appeared over the registration crisis, was to become an open breach by the spring of 1981. For now though, the union leadership tried to calm the situation down by calling for renewed efforts towards a social alliance in Poland based on wisdom, common sense, and responsibility.[31]

For the most part, the rest of 1980 proved to be a less combative situation, on a national level, for Solidarity and the Party. There were crises that broke out, the most dangerous one, in Warsaw, over the arrest of two Solidarity printer activists, but they were local in nature and were kept so due to the federative structure of Solidarity. The objective was to keep the various situations under control and this was achieved relatively well. The year 1980 ended with the dedication of the workers monument in Gdansk. At the dedication, Welesa called for peace, order, and responsibility. The next few months were to be anything but peaceful.

The long-awaited government report on the state of the economy was issued in January 1981. The document was vague at best and described as a litany of good intentions. The report outlined a series of potential economic reforms for the country. It called for the eventual decentralization of the economy and greater worker involvement in the decision making process (i.e. self-management). Despite any changes, though, the enterprise manager was to remain the person in charge with the right to veto any decision not in the social interest. The authorities still thought of the workers as self-centered, willing to put their interests ahead of the interests of the public. These were the same vague promises and accusations that had been made since 1956. These changes had to be postponed because the Polish economy could not withstand the strain of transformation at this time. Austerity and sacrifice were the keys to the future and Polish workers were told that they would have to give up work free Saturdays for the year 1981 and possibly longer. This move went against what was agreed upon in August in two ways. The workers had been promised free Saturdays and now were being told that the best they could have was only, maybe, two a month. What angered them more than this was that again they were being told what they had to do without being consulted as was promised in August. This proved to be just another blow against what little confidence was left in the authorities as trustworthy partners in a social contract.

The Poles were shocked by the announcement from the government. They knew the state of the economy and they were willing to make sacrifices, but what they were not willing to tolerate was being told what they would sacrifice without prior consultation. Solidarity regarded the government demand as an affront to the August accords which called for consultation before any decisions. The workers wanted to live by the old adage "nothing about us without us." Solidarity still offered to negotiate with the authorities despite being snubbed, initially. They would talk but not work on the Saturdays dictated to them. The workers were determined to show the government that they could no longer renege on a signed agreement and get away with it. The union declared all Saturdays work free until the government agreed to talk to them.[32]

The government, initially, refused to budge from their position. The pay of those not working on the designated Saturdays was to be withheld. Stefan Olszowski, a Politburo member, accused the new unions of sowing anarchy amongst the Polish people. Despite threats from the authorities, thousands of workers stayed home that first Saturday and an estimated 80 percent of the work force stayed home the following weekend. Talks began after the second weekend of protest. The workers were afraid that the authorities were trying to nibble away at the August agreement but were willing to make compromises if treated with respect. Walesa told a crowd in Rzeszow that they would even go to work on Sunday if the government gave reliable information and then "We can decide if the situation warrants it." A compromise was reached and Solidarity agreed to one work Saturday a month. Although the crisis had faded, the damage, it did did not. Solidarity began to question the words partnership, consultation, and trust when it came to their association with the Party and the government. The pseudohoneymoon between the state and the people appeared to be on the skids and it was up to the Party to make amends and present some concrete plans to solve Poland's problems.[33]

The authorities knew that the ball was in their court and they had to do something or lose complete control of the situation. Even Mieczyslaw Rakowski, editor of *Polityka*, argued that the government must stop presenting society with *fait accompli* and treat it with respect. A fresh start was needed and on February 11, 1981 it came.

Jozef Pinkowski stepped down that day as Prime Minister. Pinkowski was replaced with Wojciech Jaruzelski, an army general with some respect among the population. He had been described as a Pole first and a communist second. Poles have traditionally put great trust in their military leaders dating back to King Jan Sobieski and most recently Jozef Pilsudski. The majority of the people hoped that Jaruzelski would fall into this tradition. Upon taking office, Jaruzelski called for a ninety day moratorium on strikes to give the new government a chance to stabilize the situation in Poland and prepare concrete reform proposals. He also set up a permanent commission to deal with government-union relations headed by Rakowski. Solidarity greeted the governmental changes with some optimism and agreed to the proposed truce as long as the authorities kept their promises. The union saw the Jaruzelski government as a potentially strong and reliable partner and they were willing to give it the benefit of a doubt.[34]

As a show of good faith between the workers and the government, Walesa and Jaruzelski met on March 10 in Warsaw. They agreed to cooperate and hold regular discussions to improve the flow of information between each side. It was at this time that the Prime Minister asked Solidarity to become an active partner in the renewal process going on in Poland. Walesa politely declined not wishing to be coopted into the system before any significant changes had been introduced. The meeting between the two leaders gave the impression that a quiet and calm dialogue was finally getting under way in Poland. This impression proved to be illusionary.[35]

The illusory bubble burst on March 19, 1981 in the city of Bydgoszcz. The People's Council of the region had agreed to discuss the possibility of recognizing a farmers' union, Rural Solidarity, at its meeting on that day. A contingent of farmer activists with supporters from the local Solidarity branch attended the meeting in the hope of presenting a case for their existence as a union. But before the farmers could speak the authorities called an end to the meeting. The farmers and their supporters refused to leave the Party headquarters until they had composed a letter of protest to the Council over this crude tactic of censorship and demanded another opportunity to present their case. The situation quickly turned into a sit-in protest. The people were asked to vacate the building but refused to do so until they were given a chance to be heard. After several more attempts to persuade the protesters to leave failed, the local militia was brought in to clear the building. Most of the people were allowed to leave with only slight harassment, but the leaders of the protest were forced to run a "path of health" set up by the security police. Three of the men were so badly beaten that they had to be hospitalized. Solidarity had been willing to overlook many minor attacks on the union and its personnel but could not ignore such a blatant and vicious attack on representatives of Solidarity.[36]

Most Poles put the blame for the attack on Party hardliners who were trying to provoke a violent response from Solidarity. It was assumed that Tadeusz Grabski and Stefan Olszowski were the instigators of the assault. Local Party organizations from throughout the country sent letters of protest over the beatings to Warsaw demanding an investigation and punishment for those involved. Stefan Bratkowski, head of the Writer's Union, accused the hardliners of standing only for confrontation and disinformation. The Bydgoszcz beatings were to fracture the Party even more than it had been before.[37]

The National Coordinating Committee (KKP) of Solidarity met on March 23, in Bydgoszcz, to decide the specific response of the union to the altercation. The meeting proved to be a struggle between the moderates and the radicals in the union. The radical faction, using Karol Modzelewski as its spokesperson, demanded an all out general strike as quickly as possible to show the workers' outrage and unity in the face of such a vicious attack. The moderates, headed by Walesa, were calling for a four-hour warning strike to be followed by negotiations with the authorities and if this failed to get satisfactory results, then a general strike would be called. Walesa and his advisors feared that an immediate general strike might lead to an insurrection and bloodshed. Modzelweski disregarded these fears and argued that a gauntlet had been thrown down and it was up to Solidarity to pick it up. It appeared that the radicals had the upper hand until Walesa refused to accept their position and threatened to resign if a general strike was adopted without a chance for dialogue. The KKP accepted the moderate view under Walesa's threats. The problem of factionalism was not settled, though, and was to resurface again after the crisis had passed. For the present, a call went out for a four-hour warning strike for March 27 and for the opening of talks with the authorities. Near the end of the meeting of the KKP on March 24, the Lublin representative addressed the audience with a very appropriate description of the general mood of the union "we are now entering a state of war."[38]

Mobilization of the workers after Bydgoszcz was swift and effective. The people prepared as if going to war. Factories were decked out in red and white, the national colors. Strikers wore red and white arm bands reminiscent of the soldiers of the Warsaw Uprising of 1944. Strike posters cropped up everywhere. Every regional interfactory union committee moved to a large enterprise in its area for the duration of the strike. Food and provisions were stockpiled in factories as if preparing for a state of siege. The workers were ready and prepared to stand by their union.[39]

Talks between Solidarity and the authorities began on March 25. The negotiating teams were headed by Lech Walesa and Mieczyslaw Rakowski. The first meeting did not go easily. Rakowski accused Solidarity of waging a holy war against the people's power while he was told that the workers did not trust him or the government to fulfill its promises. The talks adjourned with no positive results.[40]

The four-hour warning strike went into effect as scheduled. All of Poland came to a stop. Only necessary services were kept going and even these workers wore red and white arm bands. Party members joined the strike despite orders to the contrary from Warsaw. This was not only a show of union unity but also Polish unity. The strike was carried out in an atmosphere of calm, order, and dignity.[41]

Talks between Walesa and Rakowski began again on March 27 and continued into the next day. The dialogue this time went much smoother. Rakowski even said that he saw room for compromise. The outcome of the talks rested on the declaration to be issued by the Party Central Committee that Sunday. The report criticized the behavior of the local authorities and the militia and called for the resignation of the Bydgoszcz Party chairman. It deplored the beatings and ordered an intense investigation into the incident. The government also agreed to study the possibility of recognizing Rural Solidarity and an amnesty for those accused of opposition activity. Rakowski presented the government's offer one hour before the general strike was to go into effect. There were no guarantees. Walesa was faced with a tough decision. Either he could suspend the strike on his own accord, since their was no time for a vote by the union at large, or go through with the strike and take the chance of a bloody insurrection. Walesa agreed to a hasty solution to avoid bloodshed. The general strike was suspended on Walesa's initiative. Although the crisis in Bydgoszcz was technically over, the crisis in Solidarity was about to resurface.[42]

Chapter Five

To Mix Fire and Water

The bruises from the Bydgoszcz beatings had barely started to heal when new problems arose for Solidarity and the Party. Solidarity and the Party began to split into noticeable factions. Factions had always existed in both organizations but they became more pronounced than ever before. The Party began to split into a moderate-reform faction and a conservative faction. Solidarity began to split into moderates and radicals. The moderates were led by Walesa. His group remained willing and open to negotiate and make tactical compromises. The radicals were led by Karol Modzelewski, Solidarity spokesman and dissident, and Andrzej Gwiazda, a founding member of the Free Trade Union Movement in Poland. The radicals began to press for less talk and more action. They argued that the union federation was far to passive when it came to solving Poland's economic problems and far too submissive in dealing with attacks from the Party, such as in Bydgoszcz. The radicals pushed for more confrontation and less negotiations. Walesa and his faction desperately tried to hold on to the moderate path of give and take but began to lose ground after the spring of 1981. The Party was throwing more and more obstacles in front of the union and showed a lack of will to cooperate as a partner in solving Poland's ills. Walesa was forced closer and closer to the radical position because of the inability or the unwillingness of the Party to solve Poland's economic and social problems.

The radical faction of Solidarity began to take shape soon after the suspension of the general strike on March 30. Walesa called a two-day meeting of the Coordinating Committee to discuss the agreement reached between him and Rakowski. Walesa and his advisors were attacked for compromising too much and receiving too little in return. Walesa desperately tried to convince the Committee that what he did in signing the agreement was the best thing for the Union and for Poland. He stated emphatically that he was not willing to risk bloodshed for the sake of pressing the party harder for more concessions with a general strike. The radicals did not listen to his arguments. Karol Modzelewski led the radical assault on Walesa and the moderates. Modzelewski argued that the agreement solved nothing and failed to gain any concessions on political prisoners or rural Solidarity. He accused Walesa of assuming too much power. He called Walesa a king and his experts the court while the rest of the union was just there for support. Modzelewski feared that signing an agreement for the union without prior consultation with elected union representatives was only the first step toward the death of union democracy. He also voiced his fears over the growing influence of the advisors over Walesa and the decision-making process. He specifically named Bronislaw Geremek, Tadeusz Mazowiecki, and Wladyslaw Sila-Nowicki as the primary underminers of union democracy. He feared that soon Walesa would become a puppet king with his court advisors actually governing. This privy council was responsible for union decisions being made behind the backs of elected union officials. Modzelewski gave the impression in his speech that he was jealous of those close to Walesa and that he was angry that he did not have more power. He wanted the union to be less conciliatory and more confrontational. Modzelewski resigned his position as spokesman for Solidarity to show his disgust for Walesa and to carry on the fight for a more "active" union outside of the coordinating commission. Andrzej Gwiazda picked up the argument against Walesa, after Modzelweski left, and also offered to resign. Walesa was able to talk Gwiazda out of leaving. Although Walesa remained as recognized leader of the union after the meeting ended, his position had been weakened. A strong radical faction within the union became more active after the commission meeting. They were to make further negotiations with the Party more and more difficult.[1]

The union leadership tried to answer the growing call for greater participation in solving Poland's economic problems when they issued a position paper in mid-April. *Tygodnik Solidarnosc* published, on April 17, the "Direction of the Operation of Solidarity in the Current Situation." It was a program of 'action' for the union presented to the rank and file for discussion. The paper presented a variety of ways in which Solidarity could become a more active participant in solving Poland's problems without threatening the guiding role of the Party in the state and not being coopted into the existing system. The paper placed the blame for Poland's situation on the existing political and economic system in Poland. A restructuring of the economic system would be necessary for long-lasting change. These changes would involve the introduction of market mechanisms and the recognition of authentic workers' self-government. The state's role, i.e the Party, was to be drastically reduced. The main theme was that the primary guarantor of change was Solidarity and that there was no turning back from reform. The paper was a call to action not only for the union but also for the Party. The question was how would the Party respond.[2]

The Party responded with inactivity. The only action that the Party took was to call for a two-month ban on strikes. Walesa accused the state of attacking the symptoms and not the illness. What was needed was forceful action and this was something that the Party proved incapable of doing.[3]

As spring turned to summer, the Polish economy went from bad to worse. The amount of exports were down due to work free Saturdays which meant a decrease in hard currency. Inflation was up due to wage increases. Throughout the entire Polish economy there was too much money chasing too few products. The growing lack of food became a sore point to the average Pole. "A hungry Pole is an angry Pole." Food rationing was begun in April and by July had proven an utter failure. There was no food to buy, even with coupons. The staples of meat, butter, sugar, and flour became luxuries. Even hospitals could not supply meals to their patients, who had to rely on visiting friends and relatives for food. Kazimierz Brandys, the writer, returned home after seven months in the West and could not believe that food supplies had almost disappeared and that there was actual talk of hunger. He wondered how long people could live on "pure spirit." Tempers grew hotter as the temperature grew warmer. Hunger marches became endemic. The protests were often organized by local Solidarity branches as a way to release tensions. The placards of the marchers stated the feeling of most Poles: "We are tired of being hungry." The government response was to raise food prices in July.[4]

The union leadership approached the government with a plan for even more active cooperation after the price hikes. Solidarity agreed to support these necessary price increases in exchange for information on food supplies in the country and more input on the distribution of food to make sure all were getting their fair share. Rakowski, the government negotiator, dismissed the proposals as ridiculous and nothing more than a mere grab for power. Rakowski proposed a mere advisory position for Solidarity rather than an active partnership. There was to be no sharing of power. The union leadership turned down the counter proposal. Rakowski was furious and accused the union of slandering the state and told them it was time that they started acting as a union (i.e. a transmission belt) and not a political party. The meeting ended in a stalemate. The stance of Rakowski and the government only fed the growing radical demands in the union. Jacek Kuron described Solidarity as a union on a sinking ship, at a July meeting of Solidarity members in Warsaw. Karol Modzelewski added that when the captain was incapable of saving the sinking ship it became the responsibility of the common sailors to save the ship and themselves.[5]

The Party began to act as a cornered and frightened animal. The media tried to shift the blame for Poland's ills away from the government and on to Solidarity. The strikes ordered by Solidarity officials were the reason for rising prices and a lack of food according to the official press. Papers from *Tyrbuna Ludu* to *Zolnierz Wolnosci* accused Solidarity of plotting to overthrow the government through chaos. These crude attempts to shift blame did little to engender support for a Party in decay. The Polish News Agency (PAP) reported that over 200,000 people had turned in their Party cards in the first six months of 1981. Most of the cards came from rank and file members. The Party looked to one last event to revitalize itself and shore up its ranks, the extraordinary Party Congress to be held that summer.[6]

Many Poles still hoped that the Party could reform itself and the Congress was the place to do it. There was a call for democratic elections by secret ballot and general support for odnowa (renewal). One of the objectives of the Congress was to increase worker participation. There was to be a shift of emphasis in the Party away from ruling in the name of the workers to a Workers' Party. This was to prove quite a task since many rank and file workers were leaving the Party for membership in Solidarity. *Trybuna Ludu* made the observation the blue collar workers were "becoming strangers in the Party ranks." Kania made a plea for more worker representation at the July Congress. Kania's plea was answered with large turn outs for delegate elections but the results were not pleasing to the Party apparatus. The voters took Kania seriously and elected new reform minded people and turned out many of the old conservative Party hacks, some of the latter with support from Moscow. Kania went on to appoint some of those turned out in the elections as special representatives to the congress. The existence of nonelected representatives at the Congress tended to make a farce of the first democratic party elections held by an East European Communist Party. There was still hope that *odnowa* could still survive.[7]

The Extraordinary Party Congress opened on the anniversary of the storming of the Bastille, July 14, 1981. Its openness of speech, the representative character of most of its delegates, and the secret ballot vote for the First Secretary made it unique in communist history. Kania opened the Congress with a call for greater support for renewal and for the socialist system. He argued, as others had before him at other extraordinary meetings, that the system was not at fault for Poland's problems, just those who had been running it. Jaruzelski echoed Kania's remarks and declared the government's dedication to economic reform, The prime minister did warn that reform could only take place under conditions of calm and order. The Congress, for all its high goals, proved to be a failure. Attempts to set up mechanisms to ensure internal Party democracy were listened to but politely ignored. Kania and Jaruzelski both brought up the need for worker self-management but, again, only in an advisory capacity. The Party was still dominated by conservatives like Stefan Olszowski while reformers like Tadeusz Fiszbach and Zbigniew Iwanow were ignored or removed from the Party. The common phrase used to describe the Congress became "*Nowe Wraca*," the new comes back again. The Poles had heard it all before and many decided that the Party definition of "*odnowa*" was different from theirs. The term "*odnowa*" has two popular meanings; renewal and the same old thing, the Party had opted for the later. One result of the Congress was that after it came a concerted effort to reunify the Party and put it back on the offensive. From here on, the Party was to take a harder stance towards Solidarity and its demands. The will to negotiate seems to have died that July and confrontation was to replace it.[8]

The Party had shown at its Congress that its version of cooperation had not changed much since 1944 and that the possibility of any significant reforms was growing less and less. The radicals in Solidarity accused the union leadership of not taking advantage of a Party that was discredited in the eyes of the Polish people. Solidarity had the opportunity to step into the leadership that was being left open by what appeared to be a disintegrating Party. The radicals began to take it upon themselves to look for solutions to Poland's economic woes. Worker self-management of enterprises appeared to be the answer to Poland's stagnation that they were looking for and they started a grass roots movement to implement the solution.

As the economy grew worse and the government appeared more and more inept, there was a growing demand for worker control of economic enterprises. *Samorzad* (self-management) was already mentioned in point 6 of the Gdansk agreement of 1980 as a viable way to increase worker input into the system. Self-government began to grow slowly after the beginning of 1981 but became more pronounced after the confrontation with the Party in March. The councils allied themselves with the radicals in the union. Jerzy Milewski and other worker activists formed the Network of Solidarity Organizations of Leading Workplaces, commonly known as the Network or *Siec*, to coordinate the activities of the growing number of councils. The greatest support for the movement came from factories that employed over 1,000 workers; 95 percent of all such enterprises belonged to the *Siec*, comprising 60 percent of the total membership. Factory membership in the *Siec* read like a who's who of Poland's labor history; the Lenin Shipyards, the Warski Shipyards, the Ursus Tractor Works, the Cegileski Works of Poznan, and the Wujek Mine of Katowice, to name a few.[9]

The new movement often found itself at odds with the Solidarity leadership since its proposals appeared as direct attacks on the *nomenklatura* of the Party. These activists were no longer content with a consultative role in Poland's affairs but were concerned with wrenching power out of the Party's hands. The management of enterprises was to rest with its employees and their elected representatives, not in the hands of state-appointed *apparatchiks*. Managers were to be subservient to the workers' councils. The state's role in the economy was to be limited to indispensable enterprises (state enterprises) while all others were to be run by workers' councils (social enterprises). Social enterprises were to be in the majority and the basic element of the national economy with the state enterprises in the minority. Kania and Jaruzelski's plan was just the reverse of the *Siec* approach. The key to the *Siec* plan was decentralization of the economy. The workers' councils would control pay, bonuses, production, and the appointment of management. The state would be there to assist and advise, not dictate. The catch phrase of the *Siec* became

"Give us back our factories."[10]

The Coordinating Commission of Solidarity recognized the *Siec* in May as one of its consultative centers. The Commission tried to tone down the more radical demands of the *Siec*, such as the formation of political parties, and began to coopt some of their more moderate demands into the union platform. Walesa came out in complete support of *samorzad* as "a proper way to restore the health of the economy." Walesa had no intention of pushing all the objectives of the *Siec* but found value in some of their ideas in the area of *samorzad*. Walesa tried to work the middle road, again, between the *Siec* and the Party. The *Siec* disliked their subservient role to Solidarity especially in the negotiations with the government over a *samorzad* law. The *Siec* began to encourage groups to strike out on their own. The employees of the Polish Airlines, LOT, went on strike to protest the government's disregard of their nomination for general director of the airline. The workers at the Katowice Steel Works gave their manager a vote of no confidence and suggested that he be sacked and carted away in a wheelbarrow. The actions of the *Siec* began to compromise Solidarity in its negotiations with the government and made Walesa's position more difficult.[11]

The *Siec* called the first congress of the new workers' councils for September. The congress called for the coordination of the two major *samorzad* groups; the *Siec* and a rival group formed that summer in Lublin. A federation of workers' councils was formed under the leadership of Hans Szyc. The new organization claimed its tradition from the *samorzad* movement of 1956 but went far beyond the objectives of 1956. The federation reemphasized their earlier demand for the creation of social enterprises, and added new suggestions such as the formation of autonomous political parties, the creation of a workers' militia, and the adoption of the active strike. The federation claimed to represent 250 workers' councils from across Poland. *Trybuna Ludu* described their demands as a scenario for the seizure of power.[12]

The *Siec* and the Lublin groups are important examples of how radical some of the Polish workers had become as a result of the collapse of the economy in the later half of 1981. The majority of the workers and the Polish people still looked to Solidarity and Lech Walesa for leadership and compromise to solve their problems. Walesa argued that compromise was still the key to success and that confrontation would end in disaster not only for the union but Poland as well. The key was to fit Solidarity into the political scene and still remain independent. Walesa dreamt of a tripartite system between the Party-state, Solidarity, and the Church. Cardinal Glemp described such an endeavor as comparable to mixing fire and water, not easily done. The impossibility cf this task did not dissuade Walesa, who carried this dream into the first Solidarity congress that fall.[13]

The first Solidarity Congress met in the giant Oliwa sports arena not far from Gdansk where it was born one year earlier. The Congress was to meet in two sessions; the first session was to discuss the events of the past year and create a program for the coming year while the second was to confirm the new program and elect a union chairman to carry out that program. The congress acted as if it were an alternative *sejm*, a true national assembly. The theme of the meeting was democracy. Democracy as represented in freedom of discussion and participation. Meetings were open to all representatives and all proposals had to be submitted to a floor debate and vote. The whole democratic process, something that Poland had not seen in over four decades, slowed the decision-making process to a crawl. Anyone could stop the process at any time to vent their opinions. The question before some representatives was when did democracy cross the line to anarchy. Andrzej Celinski, a member of the coordinating committee, told the Congress that a revolution was taking place and its main force was Solidarity. Looking at the initial stages of the Congress one could picture a revolution of chaos. Work was accomplished despite an outward appearance of utter confusion. Working groups were organized and they confirmed that Solidarity had made inroads to end propaganda and "new speak" in Polish society and fostered a return to truth in the media and more importantly in schools. Solidarity had accomplished something even more important than this in that it had given a depressed nation a sense of purpose and a feeling of dignity based on self-worth. The Polish people were now united as never before in favor of true social reform with Solidarity at its head.[14]

The program was a lengthy document that called for the continuation of the initiatives of the past year and new ventures that would solidify the people's ability to influence the system that was Poland. The program was divided into three main categories; ways to stabilize the economy, ways to secure the permanent participation of the people in the social system, and ways to end the Party's domination of information. The program called for limits on military spending so that the money could be used to reinvigorate the economy, a new retail price system based on market demand, and a revamping of currency regulations to control panic buying. These moves would help stabilize the economy long enough to introduce more far-reaching reforms such as workers self-management to permanently correct the problems. A second set of proposals called for an independent judiciary, to ensure the letter of the law, and a workers' chamber in the *Sejm*, a proletariat House of Lords. These revamped social institutions were to provide a check on the power of the Party in the state. A third set of proposals called for an end to censorship and the removal of ideological bias in education. Solidarity had already made great strides in ending the Party's control of information but now they wanted to complete the process. The demands put forth in Solidarity's program went far beyond those of a union and into the realm of a mass movement. Solidarity wanted to expand self-management beyond the factory to the greatest enterprise of all, Poland. The movement had grown in one year from a movement for worker liberation to national liberation. Celinski was right in calling this a revolution. Walesa warned that it was time that Solidarity quit speaking politics and time to make politics. Andrzej Gwiazda supported Walesa's call to action when he stated "It has become clear that we must take the improvement of the economy into our own hands." The slogan of the Congress became "To save ourselves by our own efforts." The radicals and the moderates appeared to grow closer together as a result of the first stage of the Congress. A facade of unity was put forth even though the main disputes had not been settled. The Congress even agreed to send fraternal greetings to the other workers of the Eastern Bloc and offered their assistance in the formation of their own independent unions. The revolution now threatened to move beyond Poland's borders. The letter to the East European workers proved to be a great embarrassment to the Party which now set about to test the strength of this new found worker unity.[15]

Soon after the first congressional session had ended, Mieczyslaw Rakowski called Walesa to discuss the final draft of the controversial workers' rights bill. Rakowski called for a meeting as soon as possible so that the bill could be presented to the *Sejm* before the next congressional session in October. Walesa took it upon himself to sign, in the name of Solidarity, a compromise agreement with Rakowski over the bill which included worker self-management of enterprises. It was an attempt to reach a middle road between the government's consultative view and the more radical syndicalist stance of the *Siec*. The government recognized the existence of workers' councils and their right to run enterprises, but the specific enterprises to be run by councils was left open for future discussion. The bill was left vague for the purpose of maneuverability on both sides for defining what was a social enterprise and what was a state enterprise. Walesa judged that this was the best solution possible for both sides since the Party still had initial control over the situation but allowed Solidarity to redefine the status of enterprises over time. Walesa's goals were long range and he thought of the future as belonging to Solidarity. A majority vote by the presidium of the Coordinating Committee was needed to verify Walesa's acceptance of the compromise. The majority of the members could not be found and only four members were readily available for a decision. Rakowski was pressing hard for an immediate answer. Three of the delegates supported the compromise while the fourth refused to take part in a rump presidium made up of Walesa's supporters. The bill was accepted and the government had created the controversy that it wanted to test the unity of the union. The government reneged on its offer of compromise the very next day and the bill submitted to the *Sejm* was the government's original offer. Walesa had been duped into signing another compromise with the government without putting the decision to an overall union vote. The crowning insult to the affair was the negation of the compromise. The Party had thrown fuel on the radicals' fire. Walesa was again accused of high-handedness and acting as a dictator rather than a union representative answerable to ten million workers. Walesa's position in the union had been weakened greatly and people began to speculate whether he would be chairman for another year. The *Sejm* did pass a Worker's Rights Bill on September 25 and to its credit, it refused the government version and passed the original compromise as signed by Walesa, but this did little to stem the attacks on the union leader.[16]

The second stage of the Congress met under a cloud of attacks on Walesa and his manner of running the union. The session became a struggle between Walesa's high-handedness and the personal ambitions of regional leaders who wished to unseat Walesa. The Congress accepted the Worker's Rights bill as negotiated by Walesa but only did so after much debate and many verbal attacks on Walesa, who was accused of acting in the same manner as the government by presenting the workers with a *fait accompli*. This was a democratic union and Walesa was not acting in a democratic way. Walesa agreed with the criticism but qualified his agreement by stating that there were situations that demand immediate action and cannot wait for a vote by ten million workers. The second act of the Congress saw the passage of Solidarity's program of action which had been drawn up in September. The final act of the Congress was the election of chairman of the union. The competition for the chairmanship came down to Walesa and Andrzej Gwiazda. Gwiazda portrayed himself as the great defender of union democracy and the right of everyone to have his say. When the votes were counted, Walesa had won reelection but only by a slim margin. The great "wheeler dealer," as Walesa was described by his opponents, had won again, but his powers were even more limited than before. He was not given an overwhelming mandate and the rank and file had shown their displeasure by voting for other candidates. He would not be able to make decisions on his own as he had in the past. It was now time to put aside animosity and get the greater enterprise that was Poland going again. Solidarity felt that it was its duty to save Poland from ruin and society from poverty. To show their sincerity, the presidium of the union called for a ban on wildcat strikes and showed the government that it still wished to cooperate. The authorities responded by raising the price of cigarettes without consulting Solidarity, an act meant to antagonize the union rank and file. The gauntlet had been thrown down again and the Party's response to cooperation was clearly defined.[17]

The Party went on the offensive after the Solidarity congress in an attempt to save its position of power and close ranks in the face of the growing activism of the Union. Jerzy Urban described Solidarity's program of action as nothing more than a blueprint for a coup d'etat. A call went up in the Party for an end to revision and a purge of all Solidarity supporters from the Party ranks. The new Katowice Forum led the attack on reformers in the Party ranks. The Katowice group appeared out of nowhere calling for an end to the changes in Poland since 1980 and a return to a strong Party that was a leader instead of a follower. The group called for an end to the interference in Polish affairs by Solidarity advisors, many of whom had suspiciously Jewish sounding names. A section of the Party had again resorted to anti-Semitism as a way to rally the people around their standard. The group received little popular support. Solidarity and the official Polish news agency (PAP) attacked the Katowice Forum as a throwback to the past, a dinosaur, incongruent with *odnowa*. Despite protests from within the Party, the call for purges of reformers did not go unheeded. Stanislaw Kania resigned his position as First Secretary on October

18. The new First Secretary became Wojciech Jaruzelski, already prime minister and minister of defense. A common joke at the time was that the only position left for Jaruzelski to claim was that of Primate of Poland.[18]

A greater reliance began to be put on the Polish military to solve Poland's problems with the placement of Jaruzelski in charge of the Party and the state. People were going hungry while food rotted in transit from the farms to the stores. The Party appeared to be doing nothing to stop the collapse of the economy and now the Army had stepped in to save Poland. The wearing of military uniforms by high government officials became the fashion in late October. Military service was extended by several months and Jaruzelski ordered the deployment of three thousand troops into two thousand villages to ensure the just distribution of food and other basic commodities. The public responded favorably to the placement of troops in the countryside to clean up the bottlenecks that hampered them from getting their basic needs. One officer was quoted as saying that "the people expect the military to protect them from the stupidity of the local bureaucrat." *Zycie Warszawy* echoed these sentiments when it wrote that "it was reassuring for the public to realize that there is somebody (the Army) who can be relied upon." The media did its best to encourage this belief by publishing a series of articles on major military figures of the Polish past. The two most mentioned military leaders were General Wladyslaw Sikorski, leader of Poland in World War II, and Jozef Pilsudski, who had taken over the Polish government in 1926, by force, to save Poland from chaos. The government was trying to convince the public that their current actions were nothing more than an extension of this historical tradition of military influence on Polish politics and that Jaruzelski was nothing more than a contemporary Pilsudski. This bit of logic tended to break down when one took into account that Pilsudski never consulted with Moscow, or anyone else, before initiating programs in Poland. Pilsudski did what he did because he thought it was the best thing to do for the country; whether Jaruzelski was doing the same was debatable.[19]

As the Party and state appeared to get stronger under Jaruzelski and the military, Solidarity gave the impression of being torn apart into factions. The Solidarity congress finished to mixed reviews. It had not ended on a positive note, but with a provocation by the government by raising cigarette prices without consulting with the Union first. Walesa was forced into taking a hard stance in the face of this provocation or lose even more support from the rank and file who were looking more and more towards the radicals for actions. He called for negotiations but the government refused to discuss the price changes. Walesa was accused of dragging his feet and was forced into agreeing to a work stoppage in early November to protest the government's stance. He did not want to do this but was given little choice. He was forced to battle on two fronts, the Party and the union radicals, and by November he was wondering which was the more dangerous. Walesa berated the radicals for wanting to destroy the *Sejm* and the government and take their place and become more totalitarian than the present system. "We must protect ourselves from ourselves. We cannot overthrow the Party . . . we have to preserve it and at the same time tame it and let it eat with us," Walesa told a crowd. He told the Krakow daily that he was tired of the radicals and their politics. "When the tanks move in, I will meet them first. They will escape."[20]

Walesa and the moderates tried to contain the centrifugal forces that were starting to tear the union apart. The Coordinating Committee (KKP) was fighting to keep its leadership role. Initiatives for strikes, since March 1981, had increasingly come from outside of the KKP and Walesa was determined to stop this trend. He warned the union that "We must change our methods to reduce production losses and this could be done by adopting the active strike." The active strike was precisely what the *Siec* had called for before the union Congress. Walesa also called for an internal ban on wildcat strikes to counteract Jaruzelski's condemnation of the November strike and his call for "extraordinary means of action" to curb social unrest. Walesa was determined to reintroduce self restraint into the Union's activities before the state did it for him. As Walesa put it, Cardinal Wyszynski was dead, the Pope was in Rome, and Jaruzelski was not Pilsudski; the people had no one else to turn to except Walesa to calm the situation down. Walesa to a great degree was bragging, but many Poles still put their faith in him as a man they could trust. The objective was to maintain the reform movement without resorting to violence or, even worse, bloodshed.[21]

The last attempt at compromise came in November at the request of General Jaruzelski. Hints about the potential for the creation of a coalition government to include parties other than the PUWP began to surface in early October in *Trybuna Ludu.* The coalition was to be created from all forces not opposed to socialism. The formal request for a meeting between the big three power bases in the state (the Party, Solidarity, and the Church) came in a speech by Jaruzelski before the *Sejm* in late October. The objective of the meeting was to discuss this coalition government. Cardinal Glemp accepted on behalf of the Church. Walesa informed the presidium of the KKP that he would accept on behalf of Solidarity. The radicals, led by Gwiazda, protested such a move and called him a vain fool. Walesa ignored their protests and left for the Warsaw meeting on November 4. Jaruzelski proved to be a very gracious host and offered his guest a plan for the creation of a national commission on reform. Solidarity and the Church were to have seats on the Commission along with the PUWP, the United Peasant Party, and the Democratic Party (these two later groups were allies of the PUWP). Solidarity and the Church were to have two votes out of five which gave them only a consultative role in this coalition. Jaruzelski presented to Walesa and Glemp the same old formula for cooperation that had been presented since 1958 when the workers' councils were incorporated into the Conference of Self-Management (KSR). The Union and the Church were called in to give support to the Party and its satellite parties. Jaruzelski emphasized that this was the offer and there was no room for negotiation. As Glemp and Walesa sat there listening to Jaruzelski and his plan, it became painfully obvious to them that the their hopes for reform and renewal were crashing around them. Jaruzelski made them an offer that they had to refuse. Walesa and Glemp politely turned down the offer of cooperation based on this one-sided proposal. Walesa left the meeting feeling that the final confrontation between Solidarity and the authorities was not far away. The state could now use Solidarity's refusal to cooperate as evidence of the Union's hostility and unwillingness to aid Poland in its time of need. Jaruzelski could now claim that he had no choice but to take drastic measures to solve Poland's problems. The official news agency (PAP) announced, on November 24, that the military task forces had been ordered to all regional capitals and all major urban centers. No reason was given for the deployment of these new troops. Meanwhile, in Gdansk, Walesa was attacked by the members of the KKP for being a fool. The Commission then ordered a general strike for January, to cover all of Poland, if the government failed to introduce substantial economic reforms by then. Walesa protested the move but his words went unheeded. It was only a matter of time before the final confrontation.[22]

On the day following the redeployment of troops, Jaruzelski went before the *Sejm* to demand a ban on all strikes in the country. He warned that the current chaotic state of the Polish economy would come to an end either by an act of the *Sejm* or through a state of war (martial law). The appearance of army units in the cities was to show that the government meant to keep its word this time. The government planned a show of force by ending a strike at the Firefighter Officer's Academy. The firefighters had gone strike on November 20 demanding their right to a union of their own. On December 2, the government ended the strike by sending in one thousand police troops in armored cars and helicopters against the academy building. The strikers were dispersed and the leaders arrested. The message was quite clear to Walesa and Solidarity: the time for talking was at an end.[23]

Local Solidarity chapters, on their own, began to take up the challenge from the government. The Lodz chapter put forward a proposal to create a workers' guard to prevent a reenactment of the Firefighter takeover. Walesa called for a meeting in Radom for December 3 to prevent each Local from going off on its own. The meeting was an open debate in which all forms of response were entertained on how to deal with the authorities. The proposals ranged from continued negotiations to outright takeover of the government. The discussions were a pressure release because at the end of the day, the Union chose to leave open the possibility of negotiations. The delegates issued a call for a day of protest for December 17 if the *Sejm* passed a strike ban. The government responded to the meeting by issuing an edited tape of the conversations in Radom which claimed to show that the Union no longer sought peaceful solutions but civil war. Walesa and the other Union officials did not deny that such statements were made, but tried to convince the Polish people that other things were said which kept Solidarity on the path of peaceful change. Solidarity was put on the defensive by this new assault by the state. The Coordinating Commission called for another union meeting, to be held in Gdansk, to deal with this new attack.[24]

The meeting in Gdansk proved to be a continuation of the debate that was started in Radom but now more radical than before. The calls for a truce with the government were drowned out by calls for confrontations. The debates on the virtues of forming a provisional government and the calling of general strike went far into the night of December 12. The delegates failed to see or hear of the troop movements that went on that night. Communication had ceased in

Poland. Walesa sensed that something was afoot but felt powerless to stop it. The parting words that he left with the meeting that night were "Now you have the confrontation that you wanted." The declaration of Martial Law the next morn made all the talk of provisional governments and general strikes moot and a new chapter in the struggle for worker and civil rights began.[25]

Chapter Six

Saddling the Cow

Joseph Stalin was once to have said that forcing communism on Poland was like trying to saddle a cow, it could be done, but what good would it do. Yet, Stalin and the Polish Communist Party did just that in 1944 and his successors continued trying to saddle that cow for the next four decades. What I have done in the previous chapters was describe how the workers of Poland responded to playing the role of a cow. What is still needed to complete this limited study is a set of observations on the communist leadership, the Stalinist system, and the workers.

The Polish United Worker's Party came to power in 1944 with the high expectations of establishing a socialist and eventually a communist system in Poland. Very few of them entered their roles as leaders of society with malevolence in mind. The model they chose, and in many ways were forced, to follow was a system based on the strict control of society. The leadership was willing to overlook the dead and harmed in the hope of a better future. They tried to limit the violence as much as possible but the overall objective was implementation of a new world as quickly as possible.

The Stalinist model did not fit well. The majority of the Party leadership failed to take into account that the Stalinist economic model did not allow the workers or society participation in the decision making process, that was left to the vanguard of the proletariat.

The assumption that is innate within the Stalinist model is that the Party is making all the right decisions in regards to production and investments and that decisions are being made with the welfare of society in mind, these assumptions proved to be false. With no one to watch over the Party, decisions were made that stunted the Polish economy rather than aiding its progress. The building of the Lenin Steel Mills in Nowa Huta with its huge belching smoke stacks was outdated before the ink on the blueprints was dry. The Stalinist economic model tried to isolate itself from the free market world by ignoring such problems through government subsidies and blaming the workers for its shortcomings. The workers saw very little incentive in sacrificing, after a period of time, because they felt that it was being wasted and that they were not meant to benefit from their work, only the vanguard of the workers. They became alienated from the economic system in a very short period of time.

Not all communists were pleased with the Soviet example, but by 1948 they had been removed and sent into internal exile. Gomulka and others were pushed aside for their talk of a Polish road to socialism.

Society often balked at the hardships placed upon it. Strikes and protests became endemic. The response of the authorities was violent repression and a call for increased worker discipline. The use of the heavy hand proved to be the standard mode of response to society until 1956. The Polish October of 1956 began with the repression of worker demonstrations in Poznan but did not end in the same manner as earlier protests. Due to the de-Stalinization campaign that was already in motion, there was recognition of systemic failure in the economy and society by the authorities. They proposed concessions such as worker self-management and improved trade unions as ways of introducing the workers into the system. Self-management and revitalized unions would mean nothing without other systemic changes. It appeared that more changes would come when Gomulka returned to power and reform was in the air. Two plans for economic "revisionism" were floated in 1956 and 1957: decentralization of the economy making the individual enterprise the basic unit of the economy and the gradual introduction of a quasi-market arrangement based on supply and demand.

The Polish October proved to be a period of missed opportunities. Gomulka failed to utilize the support that the workers and Polish society gave him after his standoff with Khrushchev in October of 1956. Even though reforms toward decentralization and a mixed economy would have meant further hardships, such as job losses and enterprise shutdowns, Polish society would have given their support at the time. Gomulka could have used the trade unions and the workers' councils as partners in needed economic reform. Gomulka wasted a golden opportunity to create an authentic legitimacy for his government.

The authorities began to move away from reform as early as 1957 and completed the process in 1958 with the creation of the KSRs (self-management councils). Gomulka spoke little of reform after this time and instead told the people that it was time to get back to work. There are several reasons why he turned his back on reform when he did. The *nomenklatura* proved too resistant to change of any type. They feared for their jobs should any serious economic reforms take place. Gomulka was becoming concerned that the reform movement was getting out of control and that if it went any further, he and the Party would lose control of Poland. Gomulka was also reluctant to admit that the economic system was directly at fault for Poland's ills which might lead people to question its further existence, which they were. If the economic system was an error, so was the Party that installed it. The economic system was the justification for the political system and if one was bad, so was the other. This sort of questioning and discussing had to stop. It was definitely time to stop talking and get back to work. Gomulka was also watching Moscow, and it had become evident that Khrushchev was trying to scale down his own economic reforms and move back toward the old system. He took his cue.

By 1958, the reforms had died and they returned to a centralized command economy. Rather than pushing forward under Gomulka, as most Poles had hoped, the system stagnated. Woldzimierz Brus and other economists of that period continually argued for an end to the command economy which ignored public needs and preferences. Gomulka and his advisors disregarded the warnings deciding only to fine tune the system that was already in place, a sort of scientific Stalinism.

In 1970, society again lashed out against a system that had changed very little since 1945. Violence was used to crush the strikes, now in Gdansk and along the Baltic coast, old leaders were removed (such as Gomulka), new ones were chosen (Gierek), and reform was in the air again. Gierek promised closer contact between the workers and the Party. Gierek pinned his hopes on the creation of the WOGs as a form of socialist corporation. The WOGs were to be a rationalization of the old system to create a more efficient command economy. The reform substituted organizational concentration and limited devolution for decentralization and enterprise autonomy. Central planning was enhanced by creating a system of indirect controls to compliment the direct controls. By 1975, it became obvious that the old system was back in place and true reform had been lost again.

Foreign loans were brought in from the West and pumped into aging and dated Stalinist factories and a number of new industries with the hope of exporting their products back to the West. The loans were wasted. The old factories produced products not needed in the West and the new enterprises relied too heavily on Western technology, which was expensive, and produced products of poor quality by Western standards. The Gierek government used a large portion of the loaned money to increase workers' pay and purchase western consumer goods to buy off the population. Many of the apparatat pocketed huge amounts of money, making the Party elite look more like the owners of society rather than the vanguard of society. The millions that the Gierek government had been given were squandered and stolen from Polish society.

What had tasted very sweet in the early 1970's became very sour by 1980. Discontent and anger by society again forced the removal of yet another leader, Gierek, and the creation of a new dialogue between the authorities and the workers in the summer of 1980. Violence was avoided this time and reform was no longer left to the Party as before but to a new organization, Solidarity. Solidarity was looked upon as the peoples' champion. Society now believed that it had an inroad into the system. Reform was no longer to come down from the Party but up from the masses.

Polish workers and society had protested against the Stalinist system ever since they were saddled with it in 1944. Many Poles thought that socialism would bring them a better life, but they were proven wrong time and time again. The number of discontented grew with each new generation. The people tried to participate in the economic system by using trade unions and self-management councils to voice their needs and desires. The Party only offered them an advisory role which they refused. Society wanted to have a direct effect on the decision making process and take an active role in their future. This simple request for dignity was ignored by the authorities.

Over the last four decades, Polish history has been a series of revolts against the loss of dignity suffered by the Polish people under a system that largely ignored them and their needs. A pattern of hardship-anger-reaction appears and reappears over the last forty years. Whether it was the weavers in Lodz in 1947 or the shipyard workers in 1980, they all felt as if they had been pushed to the limits of endurance in much the way Marx pictured the start of revolts.

They were faced with demands by the authorities for greater sacrifices when many felt there was nothing left to give. A request for dialogue was put forth by the workers in 1947, 1956, and 1970 which was ignored or treated flippantly by the government. The initial demands put forth were usually quite simple such as a pay raise, payment of a promised bonus, or an increase in food supplies. When the people felt that they were being ignored or taken for granted, they became angry. As their anger grew so did their demands, often progressing from economic to political. Demands went far beyond mere distribution of goods and consumer claims as Jadwiga Staniszkis seems to claim in her works. Economic and political demands became intertwined and were raised as early as 1944 and continued to 1981 and beyond.

Were the workers and society united in their view of reform? Not by any means. Beyond a few universal demands, there was limited consensus on what to change, how to change, or where to begin. Each social group had its own vision of a better Poland and were often at odds with each other which only undermined their position and destroyed their solidarity until 1980.

Despite the variety of claims put forth in each protest, there appears to be continuity on two demands which remains consistent from 1944 to 1981 and beyond. The demand for autonomous trade unions and the creation or recognition of workers' councils remain constants which the workers returned to time and again.

The free or autonomous trade union was the more widely supported objective. The basic goals were economically oriented with limited political objectives. A trade union first and all else second. The unions were to be used as a limited participatory device by the workers in the economic system. The unions wanted to cooperate with a Party that was responsive to them and society.

The workers' councils had much more grandiose schemes in mind. While the unions were willing to accept the leadership of the Party with limitations, the councils had as their objectives the supplanting of the *nomenklatura* in the economy and eventually the political system. To go from a self-governed factory to a self-governed state was the supreme goal. The councils were a greater threat to Party control than free unions. The Party recognized this in 1944 and later in 1958 when they created the KSRs to subordinate the councils. Even Walesa held off endorsing the idea of workers' councils until he was forced to by the growing radicalism in Solidarity in 1981. Support for the councils usually came from the larger cities and the larger factories where the workforce had contact with a greater number of the intelligentsia and were more open to radical ideas as a result. It is ironic that the supporters of workers' councils were closer to Marx's ideas of a worker run state than was the Party. The supporters of the Council movement followed the ideas of the economists Brus and Jaroslav Vanek in believing that worker self-management could work in a democratic-free market system and cited Sweden as an example.

With each new series of strikes, slight changes can be seen in the tactics of the workers. The initial approach was to call a strike after dialogue failed, go out into the streets, clash with the police, accept the government's offer of reform and then go home. Most Poles felt confident that once their feelings had been made known, change would soon follow and be carried out by the Party, this was true in 1947 and 1956.

To some degree, the people did grant some legitimacy to the government up to the 1970s. Gierek and his cronies destroyed what little support the authorities had. In the 1970s it became painfully obvious that true reform was not going to come from the Party and that only a free society could change Poland. The arrival of the Pope in 1979 did much to reinstill a sense of dignity and purpose in the Poles. The realization that society was the guarantor of reform and change began to take root. Groups such as KOR and the Free Trade Union Movement had been moving in that direction since 1976, but it was the Pope's visit that spread the idea to the masses. The strikes of 1980 saw a distinct move from the old trends of disorganization and violence to solidarity amongst strikers and society as well as a list of distinct articulated demands that most of society could agree on. They also had one national leader that many felt was worthy of their trust and respect, Lech Walesa.

The workers planned to use Solidarity and worker self management as vehicles of implementing their vision of a new Poland. Solidarity proposed the 3S reform for the economy—the self-contained (independent), self-financed, self-managed enterprise. Self-management was still looked upon as a cure to a system with no outside controls. Self-management was not looked upon as a panacea for Poland's ills but a way of introducing a check on the power of the authorities and a way of introducing some of society's demands into the system in a constructive way. The ultimate goal was a system more responsive to society, a democratic system.

There were and are no quick fixes for the ills that have plagued

Poland for the last four decades. Poland's economic and social ills need drastic change. Any type of reform initiated in Poland would result in a deterioration of society's standard of living. Was and is Polish society capable of further sacrifices? Yes, if they view the government as legitimate and there is a possibility for a better future. As Timothy Garton Ash correctly states, only an independent, legal, national institution like Solidarity could sell painful economic reform as a genuine program for national recovery. Walesa was and is trusted, Solidarity was and is trusted. The Party is not. Walesa never proposed a takeover of the state, only cooperation between equal partners. The response of the government was martial law and an outlawing of Solidarity. But this was only a setback for the Poles. As the tanks rumbled through the streets, an old saying by Josef Pilsudski became very popular that cold December in 1981: "To be defeated and not surrender—That is victory."

Epilogue

Martial law came like a cold slap in the face to the Polish people. They woke that cold December morning to the realization that although they thought of themselves as free, Poland was still an unfree state. Mass arrests, detention camps, security militia on every corner, and the use of tanks against unarmed strikers was the government's response to the civil unrest it saw all around it. General Jaruzelski suspended all public activity including Solidarity by October of 1982. Solidarity did not disappear but went underground where it continued to function and aid workers as well as other members of the opposition. The Catholic Church, again, became a bulwark of protection for the opposition. The Church also supplied Solidarity with its best known Martyr, Father Jerzy Popieluszko. Father Popieluszko was murdered by security forces in 1984 for his active support of the workers.

General Jaruzelski tried to introduce some economic reforms, which met with minor success, but avoided political reform. He received some support for his program from the intelligentsia, the new highly skilled working class, and most of all from the countryside. The majority of the people remained ambivalent. The least cooperative were the workers in the large cities. The majority of the workers proved mutinous giving secret and open support to underground Solidarity and far more radical organizations, carrying out public demonstrations, and holding a series of illegal strikes from 1982 to 1988.

In 1988, two major strike waves hit Poland. The Lenin Shipyards and Nowa Huta were again centers of strike activity with Lech Walesa taking an active leadership role. The strikers asked for nothing more than they had before: the right to have a say in their lives. The stalemate that existed for seven years was about to explode into a dangerous confrontation when Jaruzelski decided to take a gamble. He asked Walesa to use his influence to end the strikes for the promise of round table talks.

The talks took place in the spring of 1989. The Party was forced to admit defeat as Walesa sat across the table negotiating with his former captors. As a result of the talks, Solidarity was recreated and new elections were promised for the *Sejm* and the recreated Senate. Solidarity was permitted to contest one–third of the *Sejm* seats and all of the Senate seats. The voting was held on June 4, 1989 with Solidarity being the overall victor receiving 80 percent of the vote.

The latest stage in the development of Poland's history waits to be played out and to what end remains to be seen. Regardless of the current outcome, the struggle toward freedom will continue in Poland, living up to the quote from Lord Byron on the Gdansk Workers' Monument: For freedom battle once begun,

Bequeath'd by bleeding sire to son,

Though baffled oft is ever won . . .

NOTES

Notes to Chapter One

1. Wladyslaw Jermankowicz, *Samorzad Pracowniczy* (Warsaw: Mlodziezowa Agencja Wydawnicza, 1983), pp. 17–18; Polish Trade Union News (Warsaw), August 1962; Jaimie Reynolds, "Communists, Socialists, and Workers: Poland 1944" in *Soviet Studies* (October 1978), pp. 519–520; Christine Sadowski, "Bread and Freedom: Workers' Self Government" in *Polish Politics*, Jack Belasiak (ed.), (New York: Praeger Publishers, 1984), pp. 98–99.

2. Reynolds, pp. 520–522; Antony Polonsky, *The Beginnings of Communist Rule in Poland* (Boston: Routledge & Kegan Paul, 1980), pp. 28–39.

3. Reynolds, p. 521; Polonsky, pp. 99–100; Juri Kolaja, *A Polish Factory* (Lexington, University of Kentucky, 1960), pp. 4–5.

4. Reynolds, p. 522; Polonsky, p. 124; Sadowski, pp. 98–99.

5. Reynolds, p. 521; Polonsky, pp. 101 and 124.

6. Joseph Dolina, "Labor" in *Poland*, Oscar Halecki (ed.) (New York: Praeger Publishers, 1957), pp. 477–481.

7. Polonsky, pp. 28–29, 81, 100–101, and 123: Kolaja, pp. 2–3; Reynolds, p. 525.

8. Dolina, p. 474; Reynolds, pp. 532–535.

9. R. F. Leslie, *The History of Poland Since 1863* (New York: Cambridge University Press, 1983), pp. 289–298.

10. Leslie, p. 340; Alexander Gella, "The Evolution of the Polish Working Class" in *Solidarity*, Ajit Jain (ed.) (Baton Rouge: Oracle Press, 1983), pp. 25–30.

11. Leslie, pp. 312–314; Dolina, pp. 486–489; Wladyslaw Majkowski, "Solidarity as a Climax of Post World War II Workers Movement in Poland" in *Poland's Solidarity Movement*, Lawerence Biondi (ed.) (Chicago: Loyola University Press, 1984), p. 51.

12. Sadowski, p. 100; Adolf Sturmthal, "The Workers' Councils in Poland" in *Industrial and Labor Relations Review* (Vol. 14, 1961), p. 383.

13. Konrad Syrop, *Spring in October* (New York: Praeger Publishers, 1961), p. 48; Majkowski, p. 75.

14. Ewa Wacowska, *Poznan 1956-Grudzien 1970* (Paris: Instytut Literacki, 1971), p. 161; Syrop, pp. 49-50; Majkowski, p. 89.

15. Syrop, pp. 50-52; Leslie, p. 349; Wacowska, pp. 161-165; Jakub Karpinski, *Countdown* (New York: Karz-Cohl, 1982), pp. 49-50.

16. Kazimierz Grzybowski, "Polish Workers' Councils" in *Journal of Central European Affairs* (October, 1957), pp. 273-274.

17. Sturmthal, p. 385.

18. Sturmthal, pp. 386-391; Grzybowski, pp. 281-285; Kolaja, pp. 5-9; Polish Trade Union News, August, 1962.

19. Polish Trade Union News, June, 1959; Sadowski, p. 101; Sturmthal, p. 385; Grzybowski, pp. 278-279.

20. *Polish Trade Union News*, January, 1959; Hansjacob Stehle, *The Independent Satellite* (New York: Praeger, 1965), pp. 170-171.

21. Stehle, p. 171.

Notes to Chapter Two

1. Neal Ascherson, *The Polish August* (New York: Penguin Books, 1981), pp. 101-103; George Blazynski, *Flashpoint Poland* (New Jersey: Pergamom Press, 1979), PP. 7-9; *New York Times*, December, 18, 1970; *Radio Free Europe Situation Reports* (RFE), no. 62.

2. Blazynski, pp. 11-13; Karpinski, pp. 157-162; *New York Times*, December 15-25, 1970.

3. Ibid.

4. Karpinski, pp. 161-162; *New York Times*, December 22, 1970.

5. *New York Times*, December 25-26, 1970; RFE, nos. 63 and 67.

6. Blazynski, pp. 19-21; Edmund Baluka, "Workers Struggles in Poland" in *International Socialism* (January, 1977), pp. 19-25.

7. Blazynski, pp. 33-34; *RFE*, nos, 4 and 5, 1971; A. Ross Johnson, "Polish Perspectives" in *Problems of Communism* (Vol. 20, 1971), pp. 59-72.

8. *RFE*, nos. 4 and 6, 1971.

9. Blazynski, p. 150; George Kolankiewicz, "Worker Self Management" in *Policy and Politics in Contemporary Poland*, Jean Woodall (ed.) (London: Orbis Press, 1982), pp. 44–45.

10. Blazynski, *op. cit.*

11. Ascherson, p. 109; Sadowski, p. 105.

12. Blazynski, pp. 135–140; Baluka, pp. 19–25; Alex Pravda, "Premature Consumerism" in *Soviet Studies* (No. 2, 1982), pp. 176–177; Roman Stefanowski, "Workers' Councils 1956–1977" *RFE Background Report No. 160*; Jean Woodall, *The Socialist Corporation and Technocratic Power*, (Cambridge: Cambridge University Press, 1982), pp. 178–179.

13. Pravda, p. 175, *RFE*, March 3, 1971.

14. Pravda, pp. 158–159.

15. *RFE*, September 8, 1974, October 18, 1974, and October 31 1975.

16. Blazynski, pp. 140–141; *RFE*, February 4, 1972.

17. Ibid.

18. Karpinski, pp. 174–175; *Nowe Drogi*, Fall, 1983.

19. Blazynski, pp. 244–252.

20. *Nowe Drogi*, Fall, 1983; Balzynski, pp 256–259; Stanislaw Starski, *Class Struggle in Classless Poland*, (Boston: Southend Press, 1982), pp. 48–50.

21. Starski, p. 50.

Notes to Chapter Three

1. Mary Craig, *The Crystal Spirit* (London: Holder-Stoughtin, 1986), p. 143; Starski, p. 51; North American Center for Polish Studies, *Polish Trade Unions and the Right to Strike*, p. 10; *Labour Focus on Eastern Europe* (LFEE), Vol. 1 No. 1, pp. 9–10.

2. Craig, p. 144; Starski, p. 51.

3. Craig, pp. 144–145, Jan Josef Lipski, *KOR* (Berkley: University of California, 1984), p. 68.

4. Stan Persky, *Solidarity Sourcebook* (Vancouver: New Star Books, 1982), pp. 51–56.

5. Craig, pp. 146–147; Lipski, p. 68; Adam Michnik, *Letters from Prison* (Berkley: University of California, 1985), pp. 144, 146–147.

6. Jerzy Holzer, *Solidarnosc* (Paris: Instytut Literacki, 1984), p. 72; Lipski, pp. 98–101.

7. Holzer, p. 71; Lipski, p. 70.

8. Anthony Kemp-Welch, *Birth of Solidarity* (New York: St. Martin's Press, 1983), pp. 12–13; Lipski, pp. 106–108.

9. Craig, pp. 153–161; Starski, p. 56; Kemp-Welch, p. 14; Leslie, pp. 439–441; *Trybuna Ludu*, January 23, 1978.

10. *Time*, November 22, 1976; *LFEE*, Vol. 1, No. 2, p. 3.

11. *Trybuna Ludu*, April 14, 1977.

12. Blazynski, pp. 185–186; Stefanowski, p. 20, Sadowski, pp. 108–109; *FBIS Reports*, January 9, 1978, February 11, 1978, February 14, 1979; *Sztander Mlodych*, March 22, 1978; *Nowe Drogi*, No. 1, 1979, pp. 14–15.

13. Blazynski, pp. 350–351; Stefanowski, pp. 20–22; *FBIS Reports*, July 5, 12, and 14, 1978; *Polityka*, March 26, 1978; *Gornik*, May 15, 1977.

14. Kolankiewicz, pp. 132–133.

15. Kemp-Welch, p. 13; Lipski, pp. 228–229; Holzer, p. 83.

16. Ibid.

17. *Robotnik*, no. 27; Lipski, pp. 247–249.

18. Denis MacShane, *Solidarity* (Nottingham: Spokesman Press, 1981), p. 143; Lipski, pp. 492–500; *Robotnik*, Dokument No. 1.

19. *LFEE*, Vol.2, No.3, pp. 20–21; Starski, pp. 52–53.

20. Norman Davies, *God's Playground* (New York: Columbia University Press, 1982), p. 631; Lipski, pp. 240–241.

21. Craig, p. 150; *FBIS Reports*, June 6, 1978; *LFEE*, Vol. 2, No. 3, pp. 20–22.

22. Holzer, p. 82; Craig, pp. 149–163.

23. Lipski, pp. 355–356; *LFEE*, Vol. 3, No. 6, pp. 13–14.

24. Lipski, pp. 342-344; *LFEE*, Vol. 3, No. 2, pp. 10–11; *LFEE*, Vol. 3 No. 6, pp. 13–14.

25. Lipski, pp. 341–345; *LFEE*, Vol. 3, No. 6, p. 14.

26. Leslie, p. 436; Craig, p. 146; Michnik, p. 145; *Time*, November 22, 1976.

27. Kazimierz Brandys, *A Warsaw Diary* (New York: Vintage Press, 1983) pp. 78–91; Craig, pp. 154–155; Starski, p. 55; Kemp-Welch, pp. 15–16; Michnik, p. 165; *Time*, June 18, 1979.

28. *LFEE*, Vol.4 No.2, pp. 4–5; W. Zaborowski, "Dichotomous Class Images" in *Sysphus* (Warsaw, 1982) pp. 105–123; DiP, *Poland Today*, (New York: M.E. Sharpe, 1981), pp. 170–171.

Notes to Chapter Four

1. Ascherson, pp. 131–132; Kevin Ruane, *The Polish Challenge* (London: BBC, 1982), pp. 1–2.

2. Ruane, pp. 4–5; Oliver MacDonald, *The Polish August* (Seattle: Left Bank Books, 1981), p. 9.

3. Ruane, pp. 4–11; Radio Free Europe, *August 1980: The Strikes in Poland* (Munich, 1980), p. 5.

4. Jean Yves Potel, *The Promise of Solidarity* (New York: Praeger Publishers, 1982), pp. 20–23; *Studium News Abstracts* (October, 1980), p. 4.

5. Potel, p. 23; *Studium News Abstracts* (October, 1980), p. 4; *Chicago Tribune*, August 24, 1980.

6. *Solidarity Strike Bulletin* (no. 12), August 30, 1980.

7. Ibid.; *Strike Information Bulletin*, August 16, 1980.

8. Ruane, pp. 13–18; Peter Raina, *Poland 1981* (London: Allen & Unwin, 1985), p. 475.

9. RFE, *Strike*, pp. 109–113; Raina, p. 477; *Time*, September 1, 1980.

10. Ruane, pp. 15–29.

11. Potel, pp. 130–131; *Bulletin* (12); *Time*, September 8, 1980.

12. Ibid.

13. MacShane, p. 51; Potel, p. 50; *Time*, September 1 and 8, 1980.

14. Oliver MacDonald, "The Polish Vortex," in *The Stalinist Legacy* (New York: Penguin Books, 1984), Tariq Ali, (ed.), p. 476; Kemp-Welch, pp. 145–149.

15. *Solidarity Strike Bulletin* (no. 2) August 24, 1980; Ascherson, p. 156; MacShane, p. 52; Potel, p. 76.

16. *Solidarity Bulletin* No. 1; Ruane, p. 16; MacDonald, Vortex, p. 481.

17. *Solidarity Bulletin* No. 13–14; Ruane, p. 22; Potel, p. 161.

18. RFE, *Strikes*, pp. 14–20; MacDonald, August, p. 11; Ruane, pp. 19–26; *Chicago Sun Times*, 9/18/80.

19. *Op. cit.*

20. RFE, *Strikes*, p. 226; *New York Times*, September 18, 1980; David Ost, "Intentional Ambiguity: Solidarity's Internal Authority Structure," paper delivered at the conference of the American Association for the Advancement of Slavic Studies, November 1986.

21. Timothy Garton Ash, *The Polish Revolution: Solidarity* (New York: Vintage Books, 1985), pp. 75–76; MacDonald, *Vortex*, p. 472.

22. Josef Tischner, *The Spirit of Solidarity* (New York: Harper & Row, 1984), pp. 1–5.

23. Ash, pp. 72–74; *New York Times*, September 9, 1980.

24. Kazimierz Wojcicki, "The Reconstruction of Society," *Telos* (Spring 1984), pp. 98–104; Ash, p. 99; MacDonald, August, p. 12; *New York Times*, September 9, 1980.

25. Ruane, pp. 47 and 61; RFE, *Strikes*, p. 228; *New York Times*, September 12, 1980.

26. Jadwiga Staniszkis, *Poland's Self Limiting Revolution* (New Jersey: Princeton University Press, 1984), pp. 86 and 93–96; Persky, pp. 151–155; *Labor Focus on Eastern Europe*, Vol. 4, Nos. 4–8.

27. MacShane, pp. 55–56; Potel, p. 194, Ruane, pp. 51–55; *New York Times*, October 3 and 4, 1980.

28. MacShane, pp. 56–57.

29. *New York Times*, November 7 and 9, 1980.

30. Ascherson, pp. 195–200; MacShane, p. 57; *New York Times*, November 10, 1980.

31. Ash, pp. 85 and 101.

32. Ash, pp. 107 and 135; MacShane, p. 17; MacDonald, August, p. 59.

33. Ash, p. 135; *Time*, January 19, 1981.

34. Robert Maxwell (ed.), *Jaruzelski* (New York: Pergamom Press, 1985); Ash, pp. 137 and 145–146.

35. Ascherson, pp. 264–265; MacShane, p. 61; Ash, pp. 147–152; Craig, pp. 201–204.

36. Ibid.

37. MacDonald, *August*, pp. 19–21; Ash, pp. 152–153.

38. Abraham Brumberg, "Shall We Call A Strike?" *Dissent* (Summer 1981), pp. 289–299; Ash, p. 154; *New York Times*, March 24, 1981.

39. Craig, p. 203; Ash, pp. 155–156.

40. Ash, pp. 159–160; Craig, p. 202.

41. Ruane, pp. 146–147; Craig, pp. 204–205; MacShane, p. 61; Ash, 160–161; Lech Walesa, *A Way of Hope* (New York: Henry Holt, 1987), pp. 185–191.

42. Ibid.

Notes to Chapter Five

1. Holzer, p. 214; Persky, pp. 167 and 171.

2. *Tygodnik Solidarnosc*, April 17, 1981; Ruane, p. 150.

3. Radio Free Europe (RFE), *Chronology of Polish Events*, March 5, 1982.

4. Brandys, pp. 202-214; Ruane, pp. 217-222; Craig, p. 211; Ash, pp. 183-184; MacShane, p. 86.

5. *Bulletin Solidarnosc*, October 1981; Craig, p. 213; Ash, pp. 183-184 and 196-197.

6. Walesa, p. 191; RFE, *Chronology*, March 5, 1982.

7. Ash, p. 167-173; Ruane, p. 156.

8. *New York Times*, September 13, 1981; Ash, pp. 178-183; Jaruzelski, pp. 16-19; Michnik, p. 117.

9. Ash, pp. 188-191; Henry Norr, "Solidarity and Self Management," *Poland Watch* (no. 7), pp. 97-122.

10. Norr, p. 109; Horst Brand, "Solidarity's Economic Program," *Dissent* (Spring 1982) pp. 162-166.

11. *Time*, September 21, 1981; RFE, *Chronology*, March 5, 1982; Norr, pp. 102-104 and 111.

12. *Bulletin Solidarnosc*, October, 1981; Persky, pp. 233-237; Janusz Lewandowski and Jan Szomburg, *Samorzad w Dobie Solidarnosci* (London: Odnowa, 1985), p. 36.

13. Walesa, p. 193.

14. Craig, pp. 217-218; Ash, pp. 208-209; Ruane, pp. 224-247; Walesa, p. 194.

15. Craig, p. 216; Ruane, p. 232; *Time*, September 21, 1918; *Christian Science Monitor*, October 1, 1981; *Newsweek*, October 19, 1981.

16. Craig, pp. 219-220; *Milwaukee Journal*, September 28, 1981.

17. RFE, *Chronology*, March 5, 1982; Ash, p. 211; Craig, p. 225.

18. RFE, *Chronology*, March 5, 1982; Ruane, p. 173; Craig, p. 225.

19. RFE, *Chronology*, March 5, 1982; Ruane, pp. 260-263; *Newsweek*, November 9, 1981; *Zycie Warszawy*, November 20, 1981.

20. *Newsweek*, October 19, 1981; *Time*, September 21, 1981 and October 12, 1981.

21. Michnik, p. 121; Ruane, p. 254; Walesa, p. 192; *Newsweek*, November 9, 1981.

22. Jaruzelski, p. 20; Walesa, pp. 194–195; Ruane, pp. 248–249; Ash, p. 243; Craig, 226–227.

23. Persky, p. 235; Craig, p. 255.

24. Persky, p. 235; Ruane, p. 270; Ash, p. 245.

25. Ibid.

BIBLIOGRAPHY

Books

Ash, Timothy Garton. *The Polish Revolution* (New York, 1985)
Ascherson, Neal. *The Polish August* (New York, 1981).
Blazynski, George. *Flashpoint Poland* (New Jersey, 1979).
Brandys, Kazimierz. *Warsaw Diary* (New York, 1983).
Craig, Mary. *Crystal Spirit* (Lanilon, 1986).
Davies, Norman. *God's Playground* (New York, 1982).
Future and Experience Group. *Poland Today* (New York, 1981).
Holzer, Jerzy. *Solidarnosc* (Paris, 1984).
Jermankowicz, Wladyslaw. *Samorzad Pracowniczy* (Warsaw, 1983).
Karpinski, Jakub. *Countdown* (New York, 1982).
Kemp-Welch, Anthony. *Birth of Solidarity* (New York, 1983).
Kolaja, Juri. *A Polish Factory* (Lexington, 1960).
Leslie, R.F. *A History of Poland Since 1863* (New York, 1983).
Lewandowski, Janusz and Szomburg, Jan. *Samorzad w Dobie Solidarnosci* (London, 1985).
Lipski, Jan Josef. *KOR* (Berkley, 1984).
MacDonald, Oliver. *Polish August* (Seattle, 1981).
MacShane, Denis. *Solidarity* (Nottingham, 1981).
Maxwell, Robert (ed.). *Jaruzelski* (New York, 1985.
Michnik, Adam. *Letters from Prison* (Berkley, 1985).
Persky, Stan. *Solidarity Source Book* (Vancouver, 1982).
Polonsky, Antony. *The Beginnings of Communist Rule in Poland* (Boston, 1980).
Potel, Jean Yves. *The Promise of Solidarity* (New York, 1982).
R.F.E. *August, 1980* (Munich, 1980).
Raina, Peter. *Poland 1981* (London, 1985).
Ruane, Kevin. *The Polish Challenge* (London, 1982).
Staniszkis, Jadwiga. *Poland's Self Limiting Revolution* (Princeton, 1984).
Starski, Stanislaw. *Class Struggle in Classless Poland* (Boston, 1982).

Stehle, Hansjacob. *The Independent Satellite* (New York, 1965).
Syrop, Konrad. *Spring in October* (New York, 1961).
Tischner, Josef. *The Spirit of Solidarity* (New York, 1984).
Wacowska, Ewa. *Poznan 1956–Grudzien 1970* (Paris, 1971).
Walesa, Lech. *A Way of Hope* (New York, 1987).
Woodell, Jean. *The Socialist Corporation and Technocratic Power* (Cambridge, 1982).

Articles

Baluka, Edmund. "Workers' Struggles in Poland." *International Socialism*, 1977.
Brand, Horst. "Solidarity's Economic Program." *Dissent*, 1982.
Brumberg, Abraham. "Shall We Call a Strike?" *Dissent*, 1981.
Dolina, Joseph. "Labor." *Poland*, Oscar Halecki (ed.) (New York, 1957).
Gella, Alexander. "The Evolution of the Polish Working Class." *Solidarity*, Ajit Jain (ed.) (Baton Rouge, 1983).
Grzybowski, Kazimierz. "Polish Workers' Councils." *Journal of Central European Affairs*, 1957.
Johnson, A. Ross. "Polish Perspectives." *Problems of Communism*, 1971.
Kolankiewicz, George. "Worker Self Management." *Policy and Politics in Contemporary Poland*, Jean Woodell (ed.) (London, 1982).
MacDonald, Oliver, "The Polish Vortex." *The Stalinist Legacy*, Tariq Ali (ed.) (New York, 1984).
Majkowski, Wladyslaw. "Solidarity as a Climax." *Poland's Solidarity Movement*, Lawerence Biondi (ed.) (Chicago, 1984).
Norr, Henry. "Solidarity and Self Management." *Poland Watch*, No. 7.
Ost, David. "Intentional Ambiguity." AAASS Conference Paper, 1986.
Pravda, Alex. "Premature Consumerism." *Soviet Studies*, 1982.
Reynolds, Jaimie. "Communists, Socialists, and Workers: Poland 1944." *Soviet Studies*, 1978.
Sadowski, Christine. "Bread and Freedom." *Polish Politics*, Jack Belasiak (ed.) (New York, 1984).
Sturmthal, Adolf. "The Workers' Councils in Poland." *Industrial and Labor Relations Review*, 1961.

Wojcicki, Kazimierz. "The Reconstruction of Society." *Telos*, 1984.

Zaborowski, W. "Dichotomous Class Images." *Sisyphus*, 1982.

Journals and Magazines

Bulletin Solidarnojc
Foreign Broadcast: Information Service Reports (FBIS)
Labour Focus on Eastern Europe
Newsweek
Nowe Dragi
Polish Trade Union News
Polityka
Radio Free Europe Situation Reports
Solidarity Strike Bulletins
Studium News Abstracts
Time

Newspapers

Chicago Sun Times
Chicago Tribune
Christian Science Monitor
Gornik
Milwaukee Journal
New York Times
Robotnik
Sztander Mlodych
Trybuna Ludu
Tygodnik Solidarnosc
Zycie Warszawy